First published in 2021 by:

MARRIEDSPIRITUALITY.COM

For: Chifundo Foundation CLG

66 Mount Albany,

Blackrock,

Co, Dublin,

Ireland.

A94 AC81

Title: Chifundo Cookbook with some Food for Thought
           Second Collection

Author: Elaine Cogavin for 'The Chifundo Foundation'

ISBN: 978-1-8381566-2-6

A Chifundo Foundation Project

Chifundo Cookbook

Second Collection

Elaine Cogavin

The Chifundo Project

Chifundo began as a family project in 2006, when a chance encounter with a couple from Malawi inspired us to sponsor the education of five children from the poorest villages around the city of Zomba. As well as enrolling them into private schools, we committed to the provision of uniforms, books, transport and extra nutrition in the hope that they could in some way break the cycle of poverty which is so prevalent in Malawi.

Since 2006, each year has seen another 5 students join the project, bringing the total number to 75. This includes two at university, many in secondary boarding schools and the rest in primary, each carefully chosen from the community by our wonderful team in Zomba, at the heart of which are Lucy and Prosperous, the couple who inspired us 15 years ago. Today this programme is led by the Chifundo Foundation Board.

On visiting Zomba and seeing our students' homes without electricity and running water, it became clear just how hard life in Malawi is - especially for young learners. With this in mind, in 2013 the Foundation built 'The Chifundo Campus', a 3-acre site with a small educational facility including two large classrooms; a library; workshops for training in carpentry, tailoring and IT; sports fields; a small research and produce farm, as well as two dormitories for visiting volunteer teachers. For one month each summer, these volunteers run an intensive and fun-filled program of learning and activities to further boost our students' chances of reaching their full potential.

Throughout the book you will see photos of the students at the Campus but also at their homes where our volunteers often visit to meet their proud families. We hope this gives you an idea of life in Zomba and shows how your donations can change the lives of these children.

Your help and support enable us to continue to grow this project, and for this we thank you - our friends, family, neighbours and parishioners. Buying this book helps change the future of a child in Malawi. And I hope it may even help to change some of the meals you serve! Thank you.

Elaine Cogavin, September 2021

About the Book

My hope is that this book like my last one will provide you with really easy to follow recipes with ingredients readily available from your kitchen store cupboard and instructions that are simple and clear. By popular demand, a few of the best recipes from Book 1 are included and they are gems. This book also includes some inspirational quotations which I hope you will enjoy.

Each chapter includes photos of some of the children in the Chifundo project to help you see them enjoying various activities at the Campus and Summer School hosted each year by volunteers from Ireland and UK. You will see the children wearing soccer jerseys, using tennis racquets, surrounded by books in the library, playing with Lego, using laptops, all of which were donated to us by our generous donors.

My wish is that the recipes in this book will add to your repertoire and bring variety to your mealtimes for yourselves and your guests. Entertaining friends and family for a meal brings joy to all and this book should help you keep it simple and be able to relax knowing all will be well.

Elaine on first farming lesson

Acknowledgements:

I wish to acknowledge friends who have shared with me some of their best recipes.

I wish to express my thanks to Leanne Willars who assisted me in the layout, artwork, and cover design.

To Martha Wade, who proof read the book chapter by chapter ensuring that my oversights were corrected.

To John, my husband who did all the communication with Ingram Sparks, the printer. Last but not least, our son Barry, his wife Jen and Ben who did many tastings as I tried out new ideas and gave me valuable feedback on new dishes.

To you who have bought the book – know that your donation is going to help some of the poorest children in our world in Zomba, Malawi.

THANK YOU!

Elaine Cogavin

Parents with a bag of maize and dry fish support
as a result of our Covid Appeal.

Contents

Volunteers visiting the home of one of the Chifundo children

Starters / Light Lunch Ideas

Asparagus and Hollandaise Sauce

Asparagus with Parma Ham

Baked Camembert with Pesto

Caramelised Pineapple Baked Brie

Cheese Palmiers

Fettuccine with Smoked Salmon

Goat's Cheese Tartlets

Leek Tart

Quiche Lorraine

Red onion and Goats Cheese Tart

Smoked Salmon and Cream Cheese

Smoked Salmon Mousse

Asparagus and Hollandaise Tart

Serves 8

Ingredients:

flour to dust
13oz/400g puff pastry
1 large egg
8oz/225g fine asparagus
2 X 7oz/200ml jars Maille Hollandaise Sauce

Method:

1. Heat oven to 180C.
2. On floured board roll pastry to fit tin 11" x 13"lined with parchment. Score around edges of rectangle and prick centre with fork.
3. Beat egg with little salt and brush over border. Chill in fridge 15 minutes.
4. Bake pastry 10 – 15 minutes. Remove from oven and gently press centre to flatten.
5. Turn oven up to 200C. In a bowl whisk hollandaise sauce with remaining egg and pour into pastry care. Place asparagus in alternate ways. Bake 15 – 20 minutes till Hollandaise sauce is slightly browned.

"Happiness is a direction, not a place...."

Asparagus with Parma Ham

Ingredients:

5 baby asparagus per person
Parma ham – 1 slice per person
butter and grated Parmesan cheese

Method:

1. Steam the asparagus till soft,
   allow to cool.
2. Lay out slices of Parma ham with 5 asparagus on
   top of each.
3. Roll up and lay on greased baking tray.
4. Sprinkle with pepper and Parmesan cheese.
   Drizzle with melted butter and put into hot oven
   7 – 10 mins.
5. Serve with dressed salad leaves.

"Wisdom begins with wonder."

Socrates

3

Baked Camembert with Pesto

Ingredients:

1 box Camembert
1 tblsp pesto
Handful of pinenuts

Method:

1. Unwrap Camembert and replace in box.
2. Remove top rind carefully.
3. Drizzle with pesto and sprinkle with pinenuts.
4. Bake in pre-heated oven 220C for 10 – 15 minutes.
5. Delicious served immediately with crusty bread!

*"Everything has beauty
but not everyone sees it."*

Confucius

Caramelised Pineapple Baked Brie

Serves 8-10

Ingredients:

1 x 13oz round Brie
2 tblsp butter
1 can pineapple chunks drained
½ tsp finely chopped rosemary
2 tblsp runny honey

Method:

1. Preheat oven to 180C. Heat butter on pan and add pineapple, rosemary and 1 tblsp honey. Cook stirring gently until pineapple is golden brown.
2. Line a baking dish with parchment. Slice the top off the Brie and place on parchment. Spoon over the pineapple mix and bake for 10 minutes.
3. Remove from oven and drizzle with remaining tblsp of honey.
4. Serve with crusty bread – a great sharing dish!

This is a very sociable dish for start of a BBQ or a casual evening with friends.

Cheese Palmiers

Ingredients:

I packet of frozen puff pastry.
1 block Goats cheese
honey

Method:

1. Remove pastry from freezer and allow thaw.
2. Unroll and crumble Goats cheese over pastry.
   Drizzle with honey.
3. Roll up again and cut into 1" round pieces.
4. Bake in hot oven on greased tinfoil 10-15 minutes.
5. Serve warm.

*A person who never made a mistake
never tried anything new.*

Albert Einstein

Fettuccine with Smoked Salmon

Ingredients:

fettuccine/4 portions
4 small leeks
8oz/200g smoked salmon
3 tblsp cream
butter/olive oil
Parmesan, grated/sliced finely

Method:

1. Melt a knob of butter on a large pan.
2. Wash and finely slice the leeks and add to pan. Add the cream and cover and simmer till cooked 10-15 mins.
3. Meanwhile boil the pasta, drain and divide into bowls, put chopped smoked salmon on top and cover with leeks, and top with Parmesan.
4. Serve as starter or as a supper dish with crusty bread.

*A mind is like a parachute,
it doesn't work unless it is open.*

Frank Zappa

Goat's Cheese Tartlets

(makes 6 small Tartlets)

Ingredients:

1 pkt. frozen puff pastry
1 roll Goat's cheese
honey to drizzle
Sesame seeds(optional).

Method:

1. Defrost pastry and cut into 6 - 3" circles or squares.
2. Place on an oven tray lined with parchment.
3. Place a ball of cheese on each pastry.
4. Cut 6 more circles/squares and place on top of cheese and seal well.
5. Drizzle each pastry with runny honey and sprinkle with sesame seeds.
6. Bake in hot oven 220C. for about 10-12 minutes till brown. Serve with salad leaves.

Life isn't about waiting for the storm to pass;
it's about learning to dance in the rain.

Leek Tart

Ingredients:

3 leeks cleaned and sliced
I pkt. puff pastry
2oz butter
6fl.oz cream
2 tsp tarragon dried or fresh

Method:

1. Grease a 10" flan tin and line with the pastry.
2. Gently fry the leeks in the butter and a little water till soft.
3. Stir in the tarragon and cream and allow thicken.
4. Pour the leek mixture into the pastry case.
5. Cook in oven at 200C till pastry is cooked and golden.

The best way to predict the future is to create it.
Abraham Lincoln

Quiche Lorraine

Pastry Ingredients:
7oz/200g flour
4oz/100g butter
pinch salt
1 egg beaten – add ½ first

Method:
1. Chill pastry in fridge for at least 30 mins or use ready- made shortcrust pastry.
2. Roll out pastry between 2 sheets of cling film.
3. Place in greased 20 cm. loose bottomed tin and bake with baking parchment and baking beans on top for 20 mins. Then remove beans and parchment and bake 5 minutes more.

Filling Ingredients:

4 eggs and 2 extra yolks of egg.
1 large cup of bacon pieces or lardons, fried in olive oil
4oz/100g finely chopped onion, fried
Gruyere and cheddar cheese, grated

Method:

1. Whisk the eggs and season with a little salt and pepper.
2. Add in all ingredients and mix well.
3. Pour mixture into pastry base.
4. Bake in oven 30 – 35 mins. at 180 degrees.

Red Onion, Goat's Cheese and Cherry Tomato Tart

Serves 6

Ingredients:

2 large red onions
2 tsp brown sugar
1 tblsp olive oil
1 tblsp thyme
6oz/175g Goat's cheese
14 cherry tomatoes
1 sheet puff pastry (340g)

Method:

1. Line a greased Swiss roll tin with pastry.
2. Gently fry the onions with sugar, half the thyme and olive oil till soft 8-10 mins.
3. Allow to cool, and then cover the pastry with onions, sprinkle with thyme.
4. Top with sliced goat's cheese and halved baby tomatoes cut side up.
5. Brush border with beaten egg and bake about 30 – 35 minutes at 190C.
6. Drizzle with olive oil and torn basil leaves.

Serve hot or cold with salad leaves. Delicious!!

Setting goals is the first step in turning the invisible into the visible.

Tony Robbins

Smoked Salmon and Cream Cheese

Ingredients:

(Use amounts suited to your portion needs)
brown bread (see recipe in baking section)
smoked salmon
Philadelphia cheese
fresh chives

Method:

1. Cut brown bread into thin slices.
2. Spread cheese generously on top.
3. Place curls of smoked salmon on top.
4. Dress with fresh chives and serve with side salad.

Opportunities are like sunrises.
If you wait too long, you miss them.

William Arthur Ward

Smoked Salmon Mousse

Ingredients:

7oz/200g smoked salmon
4oz/100g cream cheese
2oz/50g Crème Fraiche
juice of 1 lemon
seasoning

Method:

1. Cut salmon into small pieces.
2. Put all ingredients in food processor and blend until you reach a smooth consistency.
3. Chill to allow flavours to develop but allow come to room temperature before serving.
4. Season to taste with salt and pepper.
5. Very good served with a good brown bread or in ramekins with a slice of lemon on top and a side salad.

Do what you can, with what you have, while you are here.

Theodore Roosevelt

A Library full of knowledge at the Chifundo Campus

Soups

Butternut soup with apricot and ginger

Carrot and Coriander Soup

Carrot and Orange soup

Courgette and Almond

Courgette and tarragon

Curried parsnip

Potato and Leek

Simple and Tasty Pea Soup

Slow roasted tomato

Tomato soup

Butternut Squash,
Apricot and Ginger Soup

Ingredients:

knob of butter
1 small onion, diced
1 tsp fresh ginger, grated
1 small butternut squash, diced
12fl.oz/350ml vegetable stock
2oz/50g apricots, diced
4 tblsp double cream

Method:

1. Melt butter in a saucepan, add onion and ginger and cook gently for 10 minutes.
2. Add the butternut squash, stock and apricots. Season well.
3. Bring to the boil and simmer for 25-30 minutes.
4. Blend until smooth, stir in cream and reheat gently.

Life isn't about finding yourself.
Life is about creating yourself.

George Bernard Shaw

Carrot and Coriander Soup

Ingredients:

1oz/25g butter
1 medium onion, finely chopped
1 garlic clove, crushed
5 fl.oz/150 ml. fresh cream
1.5 lb/550g carrots (¾ chopped and ¼ grated)
1 litre vegetable stock
1 tblsp fresh coriander
Pinch of freshly great nutmeg

Method:

1. Melt butter in a saucepan and add onion and garlic. Cover and cook gently for about 10 mins without browning.
2. Add chopped carrots, stock and nutmeg, cover and bring to boil and simmer for about 15 mins until vegetables are tender.
3. Blend until smooth and add grated carrots, coriander and cream. Season to taste.

The day the power of love overrules the love of power, the world will know peace.

Mahatma Gandhi

Carrot and Orange Soup

Ingredients:

1oz/25g butter
1½ lbs/675g carrots chopped
8oz/225g onions, sliced
1¾ pint chicken stock
salt/pepper
1 orange

Method:

1. Melt butter and add all vegetables into a pot. Cook very gently in covered pot stirring occasionally.
2. Add stock and simmer for about 30 minutes.
3. Puree vegetables with stock and season as required.
4. Pare half of the orange rind in strips and cook in water till tender.
5. Finely grate the remaining rind, squeeze juice and add both to soup. Stir well.
6. Reheat and garnish with boiled rind.

The man who views the world at 50 the same as he did at 20 has wasted 30 years of his life.

Muhammad Ali

Courgette and Almond Soup

Ingredients:

1 onion, chopped
3 courgettes, finely chopped
1 potato, chopped
1 pint vegetable or chicken stock
2oz/50g ground almonds
½ pint of milk and ¼ pint cream.
(The cream is optional, all milk is fine but
cream for special occasions)

Method:

1. Melt a knob of butter in a large saucepan and add
   the onion and potato and cook for about 5 minutes.
2. Add the stock and bring to boil, simmer for about
   20 minutes till potato is cooked.
3. Add the courgettes and simmer about 8-10 minutes
   till courgettes are cooked.
4. Stir in the ground almonds, milk and cream and
   bring back to boil.
5. Liquidise with a blender and serve with toasted
   almonds on top if you wish.

Reflect upon your present blessings. of which
every man has plenty: not on your past mis-
fortunes of which all men have some.

Charles Dickens

Courgette and Tarragon Soup

Ingredients:

2oz/25g butter
4 medium courgettes, chopped
1-2 tblsp tarragon, chopped
½ pint/300ml vegetable stock
¼ pint/150ml milk

Method:

1. Put butter and courgettes in a pan and cook gently for 5 minutes.
2. Add tarragon and cook for another 5 minutes.
3. Add the stock, bring to the boil, cover and cook 15 minutes.
4. Add the milk and blend till smooth. Season to taste.
5. Reheat gently and serve.

If you cannot feed a hundred people, just feed one.

Mother Teresa of Calcutta

Curried Parsnip Soup

Ingredients:

3 medium parsnips
3 oz/75g butter
2 medium potatoes
1 tblsp flour
1 clove garlic, minced
1 tsp curry powder
2 pints chicken stock
salt/pepper
¼ pint cream (optional) or milk
1 onion

Method:

1. Slice all vegetables in small slices.
2. Melt butter in saucepan and sauté vegetables in covered pot until soft, not brown.
3. Stir in curry powder and flour – cook for 5 minutes.
4. Add chicken stock. Bring to the boil. Cover and cook for 20 mins.
5. Puree soup. Add cream or milk and check soup for seasoning.

*If more of us valued food and cheer
and song above hoarded gold,
it would be a merrier world.*

J.R.R. Tolkien

Potato and Leek Soup

Ingredients:

4 medium leeks
2 pints vegetable stock
1 small onion
salt/pepper
3 medium potatoes
2-3 tblsp cream
1oz butter

Method:

1. Lightly sweat chopped vegetables in butter till soft not coloured.
2. Add stock and simmer for about 45 minutes.
3. Blend, taste, season and reheat. Add cream before serving.

The environment is on loan to each generation, which must then hand it on to the next.

Pope Francis (LS 2015)

Simple & Tasty Pea Soup

Ingredients:

2oz/50g butter
1 small onion finely diced
1 leek, finely diced
1 stick celery, finely diced
1½pt/850ml chicken stock
1¼ lb/550g frozen peas

Method:

1. Melt butter in a pan and add onion, leek and celery, cook gently for about 10 mins. until soft and transparent.
2. Add the stock and simmer for 5 minutes.
3. Add the peas, bring back to the boil, and simmer for another 3-4 minutes until peas are just tender.
4. Blend until smooth and season to taste.

Success without honour is an unseasoned dish: it will satisfy your hunger, but it won't taste good.

Joe Paterno

Slow Roasted Tomato and Basil Soup

Ingredients:

2lbs/1kg tomatoes, halved
1 red pepper, cut into strips
1 red onion, cut in wedges
2 cloves garlic, unpeeled
2 tblsp olive oil
2 tblsp balsamic vinegar
1 tsp caster sugar
¾ pint/450ml vegetable stock
1oz/10g basil leaves, chopped

Method:

1. Preheat oven to 170C.
2. In a roasting tin, place tomatoes cut side up with red pepper, onion and garlic.
3. Drizzle with olive oil and balsamic vinegar, sprinkle with sugar and roast for 1 hour.
4. Peel the roasted garlic and put all into a pot, add the stock and basil and bring to boil.
5. Blend till smooth, season and serve.

Real education should educate us out of self into something far finer: into a selflessness which links us with all humanity.

Lady Nancy Astor

Tomato Soup

Ingredients:

2 tins chopped tomatoes
2 tsp sugar
1 tin tomato puree
2 tins chicken stock
2 smoked rashers (optional)
2 cloves garlic, minced
2 tsp dried basil or bunch of fresh chopped

Method:

1. Fry the finely chopped rashers in own juice.
2. Add garlic and fry till cooked.
3. Pour on tomatoes, tomato puree, sugar and stock.
4. Bring to the boil and simmer for 30 minutes.
5. Add the basil, blend, taste and season

This is a very healthy soup, low in calories and tasty!

Kind words are short and easy to speak, but their echoes are truly endless.

Mother Teresa of Calcutta

First farmers at the Campus

Salads

Bacon Devilled Eggs

Beetroot Salad

Broccoli, Tomato and Feta Salad

Chicken and Pasta Salad

Chickpea and Roasted Pepper Salad

Coleslaw

Colourful Couscous Salad

Curried Eggs

Curried Rice

Light and Fruity Salads

Penne and Sundried Tomato Salad

Potato Salad with Mint

Red Cabbage with Bacon

Summer Salad

Three Bean Salad

Bacon Devilled Eggs

Ingredients:

10 hardboiled eggs
2 tblsp mayonnaise
1 tblsp chopped chives
1 tblsp Dijon mustard
5 slices streaky bacon/fried till crisp and chopped finely

Method:

1. Cut eggs in half and scoop out yolk and place in food processor or mash with a fork.
2. Add mayonnaise, mustard and chives and pulse till smooth.
3. Fill eggs with mixture and sprinkle with cooled chopped bacon.

*Education is the kindling of a flame,
not the filling of a vessel.*

Socrates

Beetroot Salad

Ingredients:

1lb/450g ready cooked or pickled beetroot, drained
6oz/175g Greek yogurt
1oz/25g flaked almonds, toasted

Method:

1. Drain beetroot well and chop into cubes.
2. Combine with yogurt and half the almonds.
3. Sprinkle remaining almonds on top to garnish.

*Life does not change by chance,
it gets better by change.*

Richard Rohr

Broccoli, Tomato and Feta Salad

Ingredients:

1 medium head of broccoli, washed
4oz/100g Feta cheese
8oz/225g cherry tomatoes
French dressing

Method:

1. Cut the broccoli into bite size pieces and place in a bowl.
2. Halve the cherry tomatoes and add.
3. Cut the Feta cheese into small cubes and add.
4. Gently stir in the French dressing and serve.

A life spent making mistakes is not only more honourable, but more useful than a life spent doing nothing.

George Bernard Shaw

Chicken and Pasta Salad

Ingredients:

2 cups tri-colour pasta twists.
2 tblsp pesto
I tblsp olive oil
1 beef tomato or 2 large tomatoes
8oz/225g cooked French beans
12 stoned black olives
12oz/350g cooked chicken, chopped
salt/pepper
fresh basil to garnish

Method:

1. Cook pasta and rinse well.
2. Mix pasta with pesto and olive oil. Allow to cool.
3. Peel tomato and chop in small cubes
4. Cut French beans into bite size pieces.
   Add tomatoes, olives, beans and chicken to pasta –
   Toss together and transfer to serving dish.
5. Garnish with basil.

Live as if you were to die tomorrow,
Learn as if you were to live forever.

Mahatma Gandhi

Chickpea and Roasted
Red Pepper Salad

Ingredients:

3 red peppers, cut in strips
6 tblsp olive oil
2 cans chickpeas, rinsed
juice 1 lemon
2 tsp cumin
1 tsp coriander
2 cloves garlic, finely chopped
bunch of flat parsley,chopped
bunch of scallions, finely chopped

Method:

1. Preheat oven to 180C.
2. Toss peppers in 2 tblsp of olive oil and roast for
   15 minutes.
3. Put peppers in a bowl covered with cling film and
   when cool peel.
4. Heat chickpeas with remaining oil in a pot and toss
   for 5 minutes.
5. Add garlic and spices and cook for 2-3 minutes and
   season well.
6. Place chickpeas in a bowl, add the pepper strips
   and stir in lemon juice.
7. Add parsley and scallions and mix well.

Coleslaw

Ingredients:

1/3 head of white cabbage
3 tblsp mayonnaise
2 tblsp salad cream
1 tblsp Horseradish Sauce
3-4 spring onions, chopped
salt/pepper
1 carrot, grated (optional)
Horseradish Sauce gives it a great kick!

Method:
1. Finely shred the cabbage by hand or in food processor.
2. Mix together all the other ingredients and stir into cabbage.
3. Refrigerate in a covered container – will keep at least 2 days.

There is no cure for birth and death save to enjoy the interval.

George Santayana

Colourful Couscous Salad

Serves 8

Ingredients:

9oz/250g couscous
2 lemons
4oz/110g ready-to-eat apricots
2 tblsp olive oil
seeds of 1 pomegranate
2 tblsp chopped parsley
6 drops tabasco
salt/pepper
5oz/150g tender stem broccoli (optional)

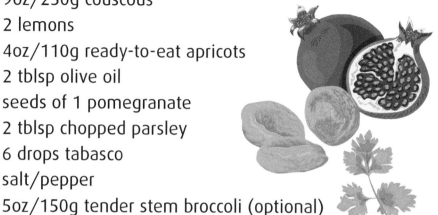

Method:

1. Place couscous in a bowl. Add the grated zest of 1 lemon along with the juice of both lemons. Add a generous half pint boiling water. Cover and leave to soak until all water has been absorbed, about 4 minutes. Fluff up with a fork, allow to cool, season.
2. Snip apricots into small pieces and add to couscous with parsley and pomegranate seeds. Add tabasco and olive oil and check seasoning.
3. Cook broccoli very lightly, leaving a good bite. Plunge into cold water to cool, drain well and add to couscous just before serving. This is a very tasty and colourful salad!

Life is a great big canvas,
throw all the paint you can at it.

Danny Kaye

Curried Eggs

Ingredients:

6 hardboiled eggs
3 tblsp mayonnaise
½ - 1 tsp curry powder
salt

Method:

1. Cut eggs in half and scoop out yolk and mash with a fork.
2. Mix mayonnaise with curry powder and add to eggs yolks.
3. Fill eggs whites with mixture and sprinkle with turmeric, cayenne pepper or parsley.

Nice for lunch with salad leaves!

*I attribute success to this:
I never gave or took any excuse.*

Florence Nightingale

Curried Rice

Ingredients:

1lb/450g cooked or leftover long grain rice
¾ teas mild curry powder
1 tsp olive oil
4oz/100g each of sultanas and soft apricots, chopped
4oz/100g frozen peas, thawed
1 can of sweetcorn, drained

Method:

1. On a dry pan lightly toast the curry powder.
2. Stir into the rice along with all other ingredients
3. Serve with green salad and tomatoes.

*Let thy food be thy medicine and
thy medicine be thy food.*

Hippocrates

Potato Salad with Mint

Ingredients:

1lb/450g baby new potatoes, halved
lemon juice
good bunch fresh mint, chopped
1 tblsp French dressing
3 tblsp mayonnaise

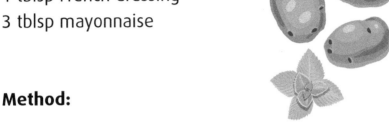

Method:

1. Put potatoes to boil with salt and a good squeeze of lemon juice. (Keeps them white)
2. When tender, drain and place in a bowl with French dressing and allow to cool.
3. Then mix together mayonnaise and chopped mint and toss into potatoes.
4. Season well.

Believe you can and you are halfway there.

Theodore Rooselvelt

Light and Fruity Salads

Carrot and Pineapple Salad

Ingredients:
1 tin pineapple chunks
1 cup grated carrot
1 lemon jelly

Method:
Melt jelly in pineapple juice, making up to ¾ pint with water. Put chunks of pineapple and carrot into dish, pour over jelly and allow set.

Strawberry and Cucumber Salad

Ingredients:
1 punnet strawberries
½ cucumber
1 tub natural yogurt
1 clove garlic, minced
chopped parsley and mint

Method:
Cut strawberries into chunks. Dice cucumber and add to strawberries, crushed garlic, parsley and mint. Mix in yogurt.

Beetroot in Blackcurrant Jelly

Ingredients:
1 large jar beetroot slices
1 blackcurrant jelly
¾ pint water

Method:
Cut slices of beetroot into quarters.
Make up jelly with ¾ pint of water.
Cover beetroot with jelly and allow set.

Cucumber and Lime

As above with sliced cucumber and lime jelly.

Carrot and Orange Jelly

Grated carrot and orange jelly with ¾ pint liquid.

Red Cabbage with Bacon

Ingredients:

½ red cabbage
2 tblsp runny honey
3oz/75g red wine vinegar
2 medium red onions
2 tsp salt
4oz/100g bacon lardons

Method:

1. Shred the cabbage very finely. Heat honey and vinegar till honey melts.
2. Pour this mix over cabbage and allow marinate 4 hours or overnight.
3. Finely slice onions and place in colander with salt and set aside for 10 mins.
4. Rinse onions and dry on kitchen paper.
5. Fry bacon lardons until crisp and bring all ingredients together.

Service to others is the rent you pay for your room here on earth.

Muhammad Ali

Summer Salad

Ingredients:

½ watermelon
bunch fresh mint
1 cucumber
juice ½ lemon
4 tblsp olive oil
12-15 pitted black olives
4oz/110g Feta cheese
salt/pepper

Method:

1. Peel watermelon and chop in chunks, removing pips.
2. Peel cucumber, remove pips, chop in half- moons and add to watermelon.
3. Make dressing of lemon juice, olive oil, salt, pepper and mix well.
4. Crumble Feta cheese over fruit and add black olives.
5. Drizzle with dressing just before serving.

The physical structure of the universe is love.

Teilhard de Chardin

Penne & Sun-dried Tomato Salad

Ingredients:

12oz/350g penne pasta
2 tblsp sundried tomato pesto
4oz/100g semi-sundried tomatoes
4 handfuls rocket leaves
2 tblsp black olives, chopped
1 tsp sunflower seeds, toasted
Parmesan cheese

Method:

1. Cook the pasta in salted boiling water and drain.
2. Toss in the pesto, loosening with a little olive oil. Allow to cool.
3. Add all other ingredients and sprinkle with grated parmesan.

Other pasta salad ideas:

Roasted peppers, cherry tomatoes with ricotta cheese and basil, feta, black olives and fresh oregano.

There is no passion to be found in settling for a life that is less than the one you are capable of living.

Nelson Mandela

Three Bean Salad

12 portions	**6 portions**

Ingredients:

1 can each kidney beans, chickpeas & butterbeans	2 cans mixed beans
4 spring onions chopped	1 spring onion
2 red & 2 yellow peppers	1 yellow pepper
1 can sweetcorn	1 red pepper
	1 small can sweetcorn

Dressing:

1 tblsp Dijon mustard	½ tbslp Dijon mustard
2 garlic cloves, mashed w/salt	1 clove garlic
juice 1 lemon	juice ½ lemon
4 fl.oz/125ml olive oil	2fl.oz/55ml olive oil
salt and pepper	salt and pepper

Method:
1. Rinse all the canned beans and drain well.
2. Chop the peppers into small cubes.
3. Place beans, peppers, onions and corn in a bowl.
4. Mix together mustard, garlic, salt and pepper and whisk in the olive oil and lemon juice.
5. Combine dressing with other ingredients and mix well.

The unexamined life is not worth living.

Socrates

Carpentry starts with a tree – outdoor carpentry workshop at Campus

Vegetables

Baked Leeks with Cream and Tarragon

Braised Red cabbage

Honey Roasted Parsnips

Mustard Mash

Pea Risotto or Pea Pasta Sauce

Potatoes Dauphinoise

Ratatouille

Ridged Garlic Potatoes

Simple Potato Cakes

Super Roast Potatoes

Baked Leeks with Cream and Tarragon

Ingredients:

4 large leeks, trimmed, halved and cut into small
pieces
4fl.oz/100ml double cream
4fl.oz/100ml chicken or vegetable stock
1 tblsp finely chopped tarragon
1 tsp Dijon mustard

Method:

1. Preheat oven to 190C. Put the leeks in a steamer
   over simmering water for about 6-7 minutes.
   Transfer to a medium size ovenproof dish.
2. Put stock and cream in a jug and stir in tarragon
   and mustard. Pour over the leeks and bake for
   5-30 minutes.
3. To make into a Leek gratin, just sprinkle dish with
   breadcrumbs and grated Parmesan. Bake for
   25-30 minutes.

*I keep my ideals, because in spite
of everything I still believe that people
are really good at heart.*

Anne Frank

Braised Red Cabbage

This makes about 12-15 portions and freezes perfectly in Ziploc bags.

Ingredients:

3lbs/1300g red cabbage
1½lb/675g cooking apples peeled, chopped
1½ lbs/675g onions & 2 cloves garlic, chopped finely
3 tblsp each of brown sugar and white wine vinegar
½ teas each of grated nutmeg, ground cinnamon and ground cloves
2oz/50g butter – salt and ground black pepper
(One can adjust the quantities according to need)

Method:

1. Cut cabbage into quarters and remove white tough stalk and cut into thin slices.
2. In a deep casserole, put a layer of cabbage, season, then add a layer of onions, apples, sugar, garlic and spices and season well.
3. Alternate the layers till all is used. Sprinkle with vinegar and put knobs of butter on top.
4. Cover casserole and cook @ 150C in fan oven for about 2-2.5 hours.
4. Stir gently a few times during the cooking to mix flavours and juices.

Tip: This can be made a couple of days ahead and reheats very well on the day required.

Honey Roasted Parsnips

Ingredients:

2lbs/900g parsnips, peeled and trimmed.
3 tblsp olive oil
6 tblsp clear honey
6 tsp sesame seeds (optional)

Method:

1. Preheat oven to 190C.
2. Peel the parsnips and cut each into 4 or 6 even sized chunks.
3. Heat oil in large roasting tray.
4. Lay parsnips on tray and roast for about 35 mins. until just tender.
5. Remove from oven, drizzle with honey and sprinkle with sesame seeds.
6. Return to oven and roast for about 10 minutes until golden brown.

On curds and honey shall he feed, that he may know how to refuse evil, and choose good.

Isaiah 7:15

Mustard Mash

Ingredients:

3lb/1.5kg potatoes
2oz/50g butter
4fl.oz/100ml milk
2 tblsp wholegrain mustard

Method:

1. Peel potatoes and boil in lightly salted water.
2. Drain potatoes and add butter and milk and mash well.
3. Season with salt and pepper and add mustard and combine well.

Delicious with Sunday roast or Beef Bourguignon.

Our concern should be not to have what we love;
but to love what we have.

Richard Rohr

Pea Risotto or Pea Pasta Sauce

Ingredients:

10oz/300g risotto rice, cooked
¾ lb/350g frozen peas
½ glass of white wine
½ glass water
2oz/50g butter
Bunch fresh mint

Method:

1. Put the peas into a wide based saucepan with the ingredients except the mint.
2. Bring to the boil and remove the lid and simmer for about 2 minutes.
3. Add in the chopped mint.
4. Add to the already boiled risotto rice or use as a sauce with pasta.

A measuring jug is vital when cooking rice, as this is always measured by volume rather than by weight.

Delia Smith

Potatoes Dauphinoise

Ingredients:

8/9 Rooster Potatoes
3oz/75g butter
½ pint/300ml cream
½ pint/300ml milk
3 cloves crushed garlic
salt and pepper

Method:

1. Peel and thinly slice potatoes and preheat oven 200C.
2. Grease an ovenproof dish with butter.
3. Layer potatoes in baking dish, sprinkling some of the salt, pepper, garlic on top of each layer.
4. Combine the milk and cream and pour over the potatoes and cover with well buttered foil.
5. Bake in the oven for about 45 minutes, removing the foil for the last 15 minutes.

Most folks are as happy as they make up their minds to be.

Abraham Lincoln.

Ratatouille

Ingredients:

1 medium onion, sliced
1 carrot, peeled and sliced
2 medium courgettes, sliced
2 cloves garlic, chopped
1 aubergine, sliced
1 red pepper, sliced
1 tblsp fresh basil shredded
salt and pepper
2 tins chopped tomatoes
2 tsp sugar
3 tablsp olive oil

Method:

1. Heat the oil in a large pan and fry onion gently for about 8 minutes.
2. Add all other vegetables, garlic, tomatoes, sugar and seasoning.
3. Bring to boiling point, reduce heat and cover the pan and simmer for about 45 minutes.
4. When vegetables are tender, check seasoning and before serving add shredded basil.

Wrinkles should merely indicate where smiles have been.

Mark Twain

Ridged Garlic Potatoes

Ingredients:
3oz/75g butter
2¼lb/1kg potatoes
5fl.oz/150ml chicken stock
1 garlic clove, crushed
salt and pepper

Method:
1. Preheat oven to 180C. With 1oz/25g butter grease a 3-pint roasting tin or ovenproof dish.
2. Peel and slice the potatoes in ½ "/1cm slices and fan across the dish in rows tilting upwards. Season well.
3. Pour over the stock and bake for about 30 minutes. Remove and increase heat to 200C.
4. Melt the butter with the garlic and spoon over the potatoes and bake for another 15-20 minutes until golden and crisp on top.

These look great and are so easy to make. You can double up quantities in a larger tin and get same result.

*The best portion of a good man's life
is his little, nameless, unremembered
acts of kindness and of love.*

William Wordsworth

Simple Potato Cakes

Ingredients:

2 or 3 left-over cooked potatoes or mash
about half the volume of S/R flour
2oz/25g melted butter
a dash of milk
salt/pepper

Method:

1. Mash the potato and add seasoning and flour and mix well.
2. Drizzle in melted butter followed by milk to make a scone like texture.
3. On a floured board roll gently and cut into sections, prick with a fork.
4. Fry on both sides on medium heat till golden.
5. Chives or grated cheese may be added if you wish but delicious with fried egg on top.

The man who moves a mountain begins by carrying small stones.

Confucius

Super Roast Potatoes

Ingredients:

12 chunks of potato (even sizes)
4 tblsp oil
1 tsp salt
2 tblsp semolina or flour
Semolina makes them extra crispy!

Method:

1. Peel and cut potatoes into 3 or 4 even chunks.
2. Boil for about 5-7 minutes depending on size, while heating the oven to 220C.
3. Drain potatoes and return to hob, to dry well. With lid on pot shake vigorously to fluff up.
4. Sprinkle with semolina and salt and shake again.
5. Place roasting tin or tray with oil to heat in oven for a few minutes.
6. Toss potatoes on tray and roll them around to get oiled all over.
7. Roast 20-25 minutes till crisp and golden.

*Judge a man by his questions
rather than his answers.*

Voltaire

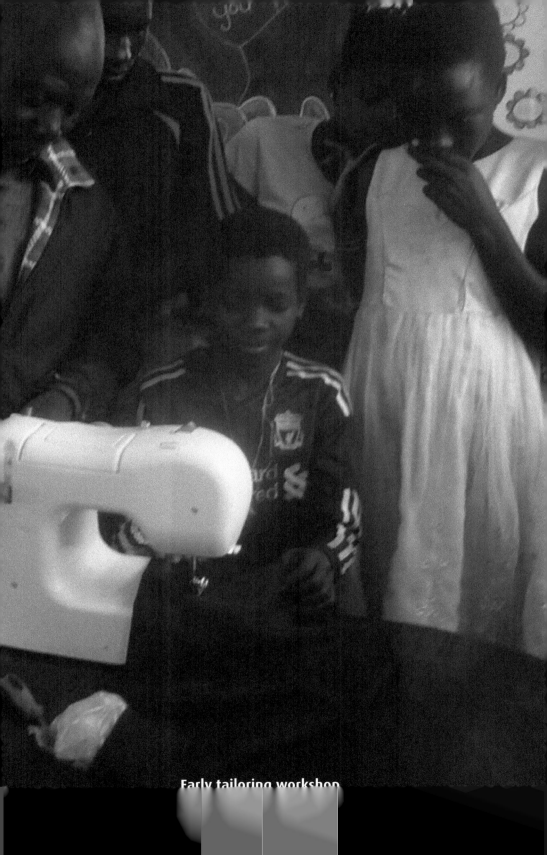

Early tailoring workshop

Meat

Beef Bourguigon

Beef in Guinness

Beef Stroganoff

Chilli con Carne

Crispy Pork Chops

Lamb Tagine

Loin of Bacon with Roasted Vegetables

Luxury Bolognaise Sauce

Pork Chops in BBQ Sauce

Pork Chops in Creamy Mushroom Sauce

Pork Steak on the Pan

Pork with Cider and Apple

Roast stuffed Loin of Pork

Beef Bourguignon

Serves 4-6 people

Ingredients:

1oz/25g butter, 12oz/350g shallots peeled
4oz/100g pancetta or streaky bacon
1½lb/675g pieces stewing beef
2oz/50g plain flour
1 bottle Burgundy red wine
¼ pint/150ml beef stock
2 carrots chopped, 2 celery sticks, chopped
2 bay leaves, 2 teasp fresh thyme leaves
8oz/225g small chestnut mushrooms
Salt & pepper

Method:

1. Heat butter in a pan and brown pancetta and shallots. Set aside.
2. Dust beef with the flour. Fry until golden on all sides.
3. Meanwhile, put the wine in a pot and reduce to about half volume.
4. Remove beef and put it with the pancetta and shallots in a casserole.
5. Add the red wine, stock, carrots, celery, bay leaves and thyme. Stir to combine, season and cover and simmer gently for about 1 hour or oven cook at 160C.
6. Sauté the mushrooms until lightly browned and add to casserole, cover and simmer for another 45 minutes until meat is tender.
7. Serve with mashed potatoes or mustard mash.

Beef in Guinness

Ingredients:
1½lb/675g stewing beef pieces
2 tablsp oil
2 medium onions, sliced
8oz/225g mushrooms, sliced
1oz/25g flour
Couple of sprigs thyme
1 bay leaf
1 clove garlic minced
1 pint Guinness

Method:
1. Preheat oven to 150C.
2. Brown the beef in batches on a pan with the oil. Transfer to a large casserole.
3. Sauté the onions for about 10 minutes, add garlic and mushrooms for few minutes and stir in the flour.
4. Cook for a couple of minutes then stir in the Guinness with thyme and bay leaf.
5. Season well and pour over the beef and cook covered for about 1½ - 2 hours. Serve with mashed potatoes.

If anyone on the verge of action should judge himself according to the outcome, he would never begin.

Søren Kierkegaard

Beef Stroganoff

Ingredients:
1 medium onion finely chopped
8oz/225g button mushrooms, chopped
1½lb/675g sirloin or fillet steak
Salt and black pepper
1 dessertspoon Dijon mustard
1-2 tablsp brandy
6fl.oz/250ml cream

Method:
1. Melt a little butter in large pan and fry onions for 5 minutes, then add mushrooms and fry for another 2-3 minutes.
2. Cut steak into thin strips and in a separate pan fry in batches quickly over high heat.
3. Add the steak to onion and mushroom mix. Season well.
4. Stir in brandy and cream and heat gently. Serve with baked potato or rice.

Tip: You can make this dish in advance and when reheating if you would like slightly thicker sauce, add ½ teasp of cornflour mixed with a little water. This ensures that the cream will not split!

Don't judge the day by the harvest you reap,
but by the seeds you plant.

Robert Louis Stevenson

Chilli con Carne

Ingredients:

1½lb/800g lean minced beef

2 onions, chopped; 1 green pepper, chopped

2 garlic cloves, crushed

1-2 fresh red chillies

1½ tblsp paprika, 1½ tblsp. cumin

2 tins chopped tomatoes

2 tblsp tomato puree

7fl.oz/200ml. beef stock

1 tin kidney beans (rinsed)

2 tblsp mango chutney, salt/pepper

Method:

1. Heat oil in a large frying pan Add the beef and brown well. Place in covered casserole.
2. Fry onions for few minutes, add garlic and chillies for 2 minutes. Sprinkle in the paprika, cumin and stir in tomatoes, tomato puree and stock.
3. Add beans and chutney and season well and bring all to the boil.
4. Transfer to a casserole in the oven for about 1½ - 2 hours till meat is tender.

Serve with couscous or rice and soured cream and guacamole if desired.

Forget injuries, never forget kindness.

Confucius

Crispy Pork Chops

Simple!
Serves 4

Ingredients:

4 pork chops
2 pkts. Tayto crisps (cheese & onion)
1 egg beaten
2 tbsp seasoned flour

Method:

1. Make a slit in the crisp bags and crush finely and put on a plate.
2. Put flour, beaten egg and crisps on 3 different plates.
3. Dip the chops in the flour on both sides, then dip into egg, draining off any excess.
4. Finally, dip both sides into crisps and lay on lightly greased baking tray.
5. Cook at 190C for about 45 minutes.

You can also roast potato chunks beside the chops.
Delicious!

Happiness is when what you think, what you say, and what you do are in harmony

Mahatma Gandhi

Lamb Tagine

Serves 6

Ingredients

1 lb/450g stewing lamb, cut into 1-inch pieces
2 medium red onions, halved and thinly sliced
2 cloves garlic, minced, 2½ cups water
1 tsp each ground cinnamon, paprika,
ground ginger & turmeric
4oz/110g prunes or 4oz/110g dried apricots
1 tin chick peas, 1 tin chopped tomatoes
2 tblsp runny honey
Salt & pepper

Method:

1. Preheat oven to 170C.
2. Toss together the spices and lamb and set aside. In a pan fry the onion and garlic in a little oil, then add the lamb and brown well.
3. Pour water into pan with tinned tomatoes, rinsed chick peas and chopped apricots/prunes. Put all into in a large casserole.
4. Season well and stir in honey. Cook for 1½-2 hours till meat is tender. Serve with couscous. Toasted almonds on top make it extra special!

This well-balanced stew is intense yet mellow. The prunes/apricots soak up the fragrant spices, and long, slow cooking results in fork-tender lamb. Tagine can be cooked 1 day ahead and chilled (covered once cool). Reheat gently, thinning with water if needed.

Loin of Bacon with Roasted Vegetables

So Easy! (This is one of the best recipes I ever got and I serve it as an Irish dish to foreign visitors)

Ingredients:

2 lb./1kg loin of bacon
8 potatoes, 4 carrots, 3 parsnips
2 onions, 2 cloves of garlic (optional)
3 tablsp olive oil

Method:

1. Soak bacon overnight if possible or bring to boil and drain off water and bring to boil again. Heat oven to 200C.
2. Peel vegetables and cut into large chunks about 2"-3".
3. Toss vegetables in olive oil and put all together in roasting tin.
4. Sit bacon skin side down on top of vegetables.
5. Cover with tinfoil, shiny side in and seal very carefully around sides of tin.
6. Cook for 2 hours at 200C. Remove bacon and allow to settle 15 minutes before carving. Glaze if you wish.
7. Remove vegetables from tin to serving dish or if you wish to further brown leave a little longer to roast. Keep warm.

Fantastic dish to serve as no pots to wash up and it is just delicious. Left-overs of bacon are very good cold.

Luxury Bolognaise Sauce

Ingredients:
I large / 2 small carrots
2 onions
garlic, minced (as you wish)
2lbs/900g minced beef
2" chorizo sausage
½ beef stock cube
8 oz/225g chopped mushrooms
½ bottle red wine
2 tsp each of basil & oregano
2 or 3 tins chopped tomatoes
salt and pepper

Method:
1. Cut the onions and carrot into tiny cubes and fry in oil with a little sugar till golden. Add the garlic for a couple of minutes.
2. Add the minced beef and brown. Add the chorizo finely chopped, ½ beef stock cube, crumbled, the mushrooms, and wine, 2 or 3 tins tomatoes, the basil and oregano.
3. Allow to simmer for 1½ hours.

Serve with spaghetti or as a base for lasagne or with baked potato.

I cook with wine, sometimes I even add it to food.
W.C. Fields 1880 - 1946

Pork Chops in Barbeque Sauce

Ingredients:

6 pork chops - boneless

For the sauce:

(Any size cup so long as proportions are the same)

½ cup brown sugar

½ cup tomato ketchup

½ cup white vinegar

1 medium onion, chopped

¾ cup cold water

Salt/pepper

Method:

1. Combine sauce ingredients and pour over chops in shallow ovenproof dish.
2. Bake covered for 1 hour at 170C. and then uncovered for about 15 minutes. Check that pork is tender and cooked.
3. Serve with rice /baked potato & coleslaw or green salad.

Nothing would be more tiresome than eating and drinking if God had not made them a pleasure as well as a necessity.

Voltaire

Pork Fillets in Creamy Mushroom Sauce

Ingredients:
2 pork fillets, 2 tblsp lemon juice
Black pepper, 1 small clove garlic
Sauce:
4oz/110g butter
½ lb/225g mushrooms , 2 medium onions (sliced)
3 tblsp sherry, ½ pint double cream

Method:
1. Cut pork into circles and beat flat in between sheet of wet greaseproof paper or cling film.
2. Marinade in shallow dish with mix of oil, lemon juice, pepper and crushed garlic. Leave pork in marinade for at least 30 minutes. (longer is better).
3. Meanwhile chop onions and slice mushrooms. Melt butter in frying pan and fry onions for 5 mins. until golden then add mushrooms for few minutes. Lift vegetables out of pan and keep hot.
4. Drain pork pieces and fry gently for about 5 mins. in hot butter turning once. Put pork into a hot dish and keep warm.
5. Measure sherry into pan with remaining butter and juice. Return onions and mushrooms to the pan. Season well.
6. Stir in cream until thick and pour over pork and cook gently for about 20 mins at about 170 – 180C.
Serve with rice or potatoes and green vegetable.

Pork Steak on the Pan

This was always one of my children's favourites and so easy!

Ingredients:
1 pork steak
1 egg beaten
Seasoned flour
1 pkt. Bread Sauce Mix
(If Bread Sauce mix is not available,
use breadcrumbs with herbs or grated
Parmesan)

Method:
1. Place pork steak on a board and cut into circular slices about 1" thick.
2. Place pieces of pork between 2 sheets of cling film and flatten down with rolling pin.
3. Dip slices of pork into flour, then into beaten egg and then into bread sauce mix (straight from the packet).
4. Fry over medium heat on lightly oiled pan.

Serve at once.

*To assess the quality of thoughts of people,
don't listen to their words,
but watch their actions.*

Amit Kalantri, Wealth of Words

Pork with Cider and Apples

Ingredients:

6 pork chops
2 medium onions,sliced
3 or 4 eating apples
¾ pint cider
salt & pepper
flour

Method:

1. Dip the chops in seasoned flour and fry on both sides till lightly golden. Remove and place in a shallow casserole with lid. Season well.
2. Fry onions gently on pan till soft. Pour cider onto pan and bring to boil.
3. Peel the apples, cut into large chunks and add to the pan. Pour over the chops.
4. Cover casserole and cook for an hour to an hour and half till pork is very tender.

Serve with mash or pasta.

What wond'rous life this is I lead!
Ripe apples drop about my head;
The luscious clusters of the vine,
Upon my mouth do crush their wine.

Andrew Marvel 1621 – 1678

Roast Stuffed Loin of Pork

Ingredients:

3 – 4 lbs. loin of pork with pocket for stuffing
1 tbsp chopped thyme
2 cloves garlic, crushed
1 tin of peaches in syrup
7 or 8 rindless, smoked, streaky rashers

Method:

1. Firstly lay out a large square of tinfoil on your worktop. On top of this lay a similar sized square of parchment paper. Lay the rashers in strips on the centre of the parchment, enough to wrap the pork joint.
2. Drain peaches and chop half of them roughly, mix in the thyme and garlic. Set other half of peaches aside. Stuff this mixture into the pork and tie with string.
3. Lift the loin of pork and place fat side down on rashers.
4. Roll parchment paper around joint and make sealed parcel. Then roll the foil around and seal again.
5. Put on rack and roast for about 2 hours at 180C.
6. Open paper and allow to brown bacon side up for about 20 mins.
7. Cool joint for at least 20 minutes before carving.

Serve with remaining peach slices.

For the gravy:

2 tsp cornflour
¾ pt. chicken stock
seasoning

1. Tilt the roasting pan and add few ice cubes to gather fatty residue. Remove.
2. Mix 2 teasp cornflour with water and add to the pan, stir while adding the chicken stock and season to taste.

This is absolutely delicious served hot and just as good served cold for a summer lunch.

Every time you spend money, you're casting a vote for the kind of world you want.

Anna Lappe

Egg and Spoon Race on the sports field during Summer School

Chicken

A Quick and Tasty Chicken Dish

Bacon Wrapped Maple Chicken

Baked Chicken with Lemons

Chicken, Spinach and Mushroom Bake

Chicken a la Crème

Chicken and Broccoli/Asparagus Bake

Chicken and Leek Lasagne

Chicken Fillet Bake

Chicken Fillets with Cheese and Bacon

Chicken Parcel with Mushroom, Wine and Thyme

Chicken Tagine

Cogavin's Coq au Vin

Chicken with Tarragon and Leeks

Escalopes of Turkey in Mushroom Sauce

Spicy Chicken Thighs

Tarragon Chicken Fricassee

Turkey Riesling

A Quick and Tasty Chicken Dish

Ingredients:

4 chicken fillets
1/3 of a jar of mango chutney
9oz/250mls cream
1 tblsp chopped coriander
The above can be doubled with same great result.

Method:

1. Place the chicken fillets in a shallow, ovenproof dish.
2. Mix together the chutney, cream and coriander.
3. Pour over the chicken.
4. Cook for about 30-40 mins @ 200C uncovered.

In my first book this recipe was the one most people just absolutely loved. A real Showstopper!

Just improves if left in warm oven when guests are late!

The best and most beautiful things in life cannot be seen, not touched, but are felt in the heart.

Helen Keller

Bacon Wrapped Maple Chicken

Ingredients:

4 chicken fillets
½ cup maple syrup
¼ cup Dijon mustard
2 tblsp soya sauce
1 tsp minced garlic
8 slices streaky bacon
Salt & pepper

Method:

1. Heat oven to 200C. Season chicken with salt & pepper.
2. Wrap chicken fillets in streaky bacon and place in ovenproof dish.
3. Combine maple syrup, mustard, soya sauce and garlic together and pour over chicken.
4. Cook for 25 – 30 minutes until chicken is cooked.

You are never too old to set another goal or to dream a new dream!

C.S. Lewis

Baked Chicken with Lemons

Ingredients:

6 portion size pieces of chicken with skin on
6 lemons
3 tblsp honey
few strips of red chilli
salt and pepper
3 cloves garlic
Oil

Method:

1. Place all the chicken pieces skin side up in an open baking dish.
2. Squeeze 3 lemons and pour juice over the chicken.
3. Chop the garlic and scatter around the dish and season well.
4. Drizzle the honey over the skin of the chicken.
5. Cut remaining lemons in quarters and add to into the dish.
6. Roast uncovered for about 45 minutes @ 180C till chicken is cooked.

Garlic makes it good!

Alice May Brook

Chicken, Spinach and Mushroom Bake

Serves 4

Ingredients:

1 lg. bag spinach
½ tsp grated nutmeg
4 chicken fillets, halved
2oz/50g butter
8oz/200gr mushrooms
1 clove garlic, minced
1 carton crème fraiche
2oz/50g Gruyere cheese
salt & Pepper

Method:

1. Heat oven to 220C.
2. Wash spinach, place in a pan, cover and cook over high heat, for 5 minutes stirring occasionally.
3. Drain spinach in colander pressing moisture out with a wooden spoon. Chop coarsely and return to pan – add nutmeg and plenty of salt & pepper. Toss 1 – 2 minutes on high heat. Spread over base of baking dish.
4. Season chicken and brown on pan with oil and 1oz of butter.Spread over spinach.
5. Melt remaining butter on the pan, add sliced mushrooms, garlic and seasoning – fry for 5 minutes.
6. Add crème fraiche and stir to make sauce. Pour over chicken – grate cheese evenly over the top. Bake 30 – 40 minutes till golden brown and chicken is cooked.

Chicken a la Crème

Ingredients:

4 chicken fillets
1 pkt. Boursin Garlic and Herb cream cheese
1 glass white wine
4 fl.oz/110ml cream
Salt & pepper
1oz flour

Method:

1. Toss the chicken in seasoned flour.
2. Fry gently till golden brown and set aside in covered baking dish.
3. Clean pan and add wine and cheese, stir till mixed well and add cream.
4. Pour contents of pan over chicken and cook for about 40 minutes @ 180C.
5. Serve with baby new potatoes or rice and green vegetables.

All that is necessary for the triumph of evil is that good men do nothing.

Edmund Burke

Chicken and Broccoli/Asparagus Bake
Serves 4

Ingredients:
4 cooked chicken fillets or leftovers of a roast chicken
1 tin Erin cream of mushroom soup
½ tin of full cream milk
1 -2 teaspoons of curry powder (to taste)
1 cup breadcrumbs mixed with grated cheddar cheese
1 head of broccoli
1oz melted butter

Method:
1. Cut the chicken into bite size chunks.
2. Prepare about same volume of broccoli and microwave in a dish with a little water covered with pierced cling film – about 2½ minutes. Cool in cold water immediately.
3. Place the chicken and cooked broccoli/asparagus in an ovenproof dish.
4. In a bowl mix the mushroom soup with about ½ tin of milk and the curry powder. Stir till smooth. Pour over the chicken and broccoli, covering well.
5. Mix the breadcrumbs with grated cheese or with herbs and pine nuts. Sprinkle over the dish, covering well.
6. Drizzle melted butter over the crumb topping and bake in oven for about 35 minutes at 190C till brown and bubbling. Nice served with baked potato.

Chicken and Leek Lasagne
Takes a little effort but simply delicious!

Ingredients:

4 chicken fillets
1¼pts/700ml chicken stock
10fl.oz/300ml white wine
1 bay leaf
3oz/75g plain flour
Salt /black pepper
4oz/100g butter
1¼lbs/500g leeks, washed and sliced finely
1 clove garlic, crushed
2oz/50g grated Parmesan
4fl.oz/100ml cream
7oz/200g lasagne sheets
4oz/100g Gruyère cheese, grated
3 tblsp pine nuts (optional)

Method:

Preheat the oven to 180C.
1. Slice the chicken into small, bite sized pieces, place in covered ovenproof dish and pour over the stock, white wine and bay leaf. Season well. Cook in the oven for 15-20 minutes or until the chicken is tender.
2. Remove the chicken from the dish with a slotted spoon. Reserve liquid to make the sauce.

3. In a large pot melt 25g/1oz butter. Cook the leeks and garlic for about 15 minutes over a medium low heat. Season to taste with salt and pepper.
4. To make the sauce: Melt the remaining butter in the saucepan, stir in the flour. Whisk in the re-served cooking liquid and place back on the heat. Bring to the boil, stirring all the time. Season well, add the cream and bring back to the boil. Remove from the heat and stir in three quarters of the grated Gruyère cheese.
5. To assemble the lasagne: Immerse the lasagne sheets separately in boiling water for about 1 minute and drain. Spoon a little of the sauce over the base of an oven proof dish. Top with a layer of pasta, followed by one third of the chicken and leeks, some more of the sauce and a sprinkle of parmesan.
6. Continue layering in this way, finishing with a generous layer of sauce. Sprinkle over the remaining Gruyère, Parmesan and the pine nuts. Bake in the preheated oven for 45-50 minutes. Rest for about 10 minutes before serving. Lovely with a baked potato or green salad.

Well worth using Gruyere Cheese for full flavour!

Chicken Fillet Bake

Ingredients:

4 chicken fillets
2 tblsp mayonnaise
1 cup breadcrumbs
2 tblsp grated Parmesan/or other hard cheese
1 tblsp flour

Method:

1. Cut the chicken fillets lengthwise in 2 or 3 pieces depending on size of fillets.
2. Dip chicken into flour, then into mayonnaise and finally into crumb and cheese mix.
3. Bake on lightly greased tray at 180C till nicely browned and chicken is cooked about 25 minutes.
4. This chicken is lovely hot but equally nice served cold for a summer lunch. One can make a light garlic mayonnaise to serve with it but very tasty just as it is.

Enjoying a meal with full awareness can be a powerful, enlightening and healing experience.

David Simon

Chicken Fillets with Cheese and Bacon

Serves 4 but so easily doubled or trebled!

Ingredients:

1 large bunch parsley, chopped
7oz/200g carton full-fat cream cheese
Salt and ground black pepper
4 skinless chicken fillets
8 rashers streaky bacon
2 tblsp olive oil

Method:

1. Preheat oven to 200C.
2. Blend cream cheese and parsley together. Add seasoning.
3. With a rolling pin, beat each chicken fillet between 2 pieces of cling film, to double its width.
4. Divide the cheese mixture between each fillet and then roll up to encase filling, with the join underneath.
5. Wrap 2 rashers around each chicken fillet.
6. Place fillets in a small roasting tin and brush with olive oil. Bake for 35 mins or until juices run clear when chicken is pierced with fine skewer.
7. Remove from oven and slice each fillet into 3 or 4 and arrange on each plate. Serve along with boiled new potatoes and salad.

Turn your face to the sun
and the shadows fall behind you.

Maori proverb

Chicken Parcel with Mushroom, White Wine and Thyme

Serves 2

Ingredients:

2 chicken fillets
handful of dried porcini mushrooms
9oz/250g mixed mushrooms
large glass white wine
2oz/10g butter
1 dsp thyme
2 cloves chopped garlic

Method:

1. Preheat oven to 220C.
2. Make a large envelope with tinfoil, sealing 3 sides carefully.
3. Mix all ingredients together except wine and put into foil bag.
4. Pour in wine and seal the 4th side of foil bag.
5. Place on baking tray and bake for about 35-40 minutes.
6. Remove from oven, slit open foil and place contents onto serving dish.

Good served with new potatoes and green vegetable.
If doubling recipe make a tinfoil parcel for each two!
Vary the recipe with grated parsnip, smoked bacon and red wine.

Chicken Tagine

Ingredients:

7oz/200g chicken fillets, cubed
6-8 dried apricots, chopped
1 red onion, finely chopped
3oz/80g tagine paste
9fl.oz/250ml chicken stock
I tin chopped tomatoes

Method:

1. Preheat oven to 170C.
2. Fry onion on a pan and cook till soft.
3. Toss chicken in a little seasoned flour and brown
   gently on the pan.
4. Stir in stock, tomatoes, tagine paste and apricots.
5. Transfer into casserole and cook in oven for 1 hour.
6. Serve with rice or couscous.

*Do not the most moving moments of our lives
find us all without words?*

Marcel Marceau

Cogavin's Coq au Vin

Ingredients:

1 bottle red wine
1 tbsp olive oil
1 large chicken, jointed into eight
250g/9oz smoked streaky bacon, cut into small pieces
200g/7oz button mushrooms
400g/14oz shallots, peeled
3 sticks celery, finely chopped
60g/2¼oz plain flour
6 sprigs fresh thyme
600ml/1 pint chicken stock
Seasoning
Preheat oven to 180C

Method:

1. Pour the wine into a saucepan and boil over a high heat until the volume has reduced by half.
   Set aside.
2. Fry chicken joints in oil till browned all over.
   Remove and set aside.
3. Add the bacon and fry until the fat is rendered, then remove from the pan and set aside. Add the mushrooms and fry gently, then remove from the pan and set aside.
4. Add the shallots and celery to the pan and fry over a high heat for few minutes.

5. Sprinkle in the flour and stir for 1 minute. Gradually add the reduced wine and stock and stir until combined. Bring to the boil, put all ingredients into casserole, add the thyme and season with salt and pepper.
6. Put into oven at 180C. with the lid on for about 1½ hours or until the chicken is tender and cooked through.
7. Remove the thyme sprigs and serve with mashed potato.

Cook's Tip: sit shallots in boiling water for a few minutes and the peel falls away easily.

What you are is God's gift to you, what you become is your gift to God.

Hans Urs von Balthasar

Chicken with Tarragon and Leeks

Serves 4

Ingredients:

4 chicken fillets
1 vegetable stock cube in ½ pt water
1 tblsp fresh tarragon
2 large leeks
1 tub of crème fraiche
1 glass sherry (optional)
salt & pepper
flour
oil and butter

Method:

1. Cut each chicken fillet into 4 or 5 pieces. Toss in seasoned flour.
2. Brown in oil and butter on a pan and place in shallow, covered casserole dish.
3. Wash and thinly slice the leeks and fry slowly in covered pan till soft.
4. Add the crème fraiche, vegetable stock and sherry to the pan and bring to the boil.
5. Pour sauce over the chicken and cook in the oven @ 170C. for about 40 minutes.

Serve with carrots or green vegetable and potatoes or rice. This recipe doubles up very well and can serve 8 – 10 people depending on size of fillets.

Escalopes of Turkey in Mushroom Sauce

Ingredients:

4 or 6 escalopes of turkey
4 or 6 shallots
1 pkt lardons of bacon
1 cup mushrooms
1 chunk of Boursin cheese
2 tblsp of crème fraiche

Method:

1. Fry the turkey in butter with sliced shallots and lardons.
2. When turning turkey add sliced mushrooms. Fry till turkey is cooked and golden.
3. Add the crème fraiche. Mix in gently. Crumble in the Boursin cheese.
4. Bring all to full heat and serve with boiled rice.

" A turkey never voted for an early Christmas. "

Arnold H. Glasgow

Spicy Chicken Thighs

Ingredients:

8 chicken thighs (no need to skin or bone)
1lb/500g baby potatoes
1lb/500g plum cherry tomatoes
4-5 sprigs thyme
2 tblsp olive oil
5 tblsp harissa paste
Salt and pepper

Method:

1. Preheat oven to 200C. and slice baby potatoes in half lengthways.
2. Place the chicken and baby potatoes in a large roasting tray with tomatoes and thyme, drizzle all over with olive oil and harissa paste and toss all together so everything is evenly coated.
3. Putting potatoes and tomatoes at base of tin and chicken on top, bake in oven for 35-40 minutes. Season well. This can be served directly from roasting tin on the table.

The invariable mark of wisdom is to see the miraculous in the common.

Ralph Waldo Emerson

Tarragon Chicken Fricassee

Ingredients:

4 chicken fillets
3 tblsp flour
4 tblsp olive oil
1oz butter
salt and pepper
2 leeks washed, trimmed and sliced
2 cloves garlic, finely chopped
150ml/5oz dry white wine
500ml/17oz chicken stock
Bunch of tarragon, chopped roughly

Method:

1. Toss chicken in seasoned flour.
2. Heat half the oil in pan and fry chicken till golden – remove.
3. Add butter to pan with leeks and garlic and fry few minutes.
4. Pour wine into pan and stir till creamy, add stock, cook for 5 – 10 minutes to reduce.
5. Return chicken to pan with tarragon and simmer covered for 15 – 20 minutes till chicken is cooked.
6. Serve with potatoes, or rice and green vegetable.

In this plate of food, I see the entire universe supporting my existence.

Tich Nhat Hanh

Turkey Riesling

Ingredients:

1oz butter
4 turkey portions
4 spring onions, washed & chopped
4oz mushrooms, washed & chopped
salt & freshly ground pepper
¼ pint Riesling wine
4 tblsp double cream
To garnish - chopped parsley

Method:

1. Heat butter in frying pan and brown the turkey on all sides.
   Lower heat, add onions and mushrooms.
2. Transfer to casserole and season well.
3. Add wine, cover and cook @ 180C for ¾ hour.
   Add cream and cook for further 15 mins – test and adjust seasoning.
4. Serve with sprinkled parsley.

A bird is safe in its nest – but that is not what its wings are made for.

Amit Ray, World Peace: The Voice of a Mountain Bird

How a small gesture can make difference

– Reflection by a Volunteer Summer School Teacher

Here is a glimpse of the last day of lessons in 2017's summer school: student Eric Phiri is standing in front of 50 or so peers; Irish and English volunteer teachers; and half a dozen Malawian volunteers. He is speaking articulately in English, calling up younger learners on how to express themselves more clearly. His hands are free of notes and prompts, allowing him to gesticulate boldly like a confident school teacher, addressing the entire group which listen attentively to his wise words. He is standing in the courtyard of the outstanding Education Centre which has now become, I believe, a profoundly significant part of the lives of all who listen to him – adult and young person alike. To his left is the well-stocked library and now occasional cinema, the junior classroom, decked out with colourful wall displays and pupils' artwork hanging from the ceiling. To his left is the office, full of resources, student records and donated stationery supplies. Next to this, the senior classroom where wall displays are not of farm animals but of high level poetic devices, guidance on how to write formal letters in English and motivational quotes with analysis from pupils themselves. Behind him is the accommodation of the talented and committed volunteers as well as the cooking facilities where Lucy and her phenomenal team prepare excellent, balanced meals for sometimes 6, sometimes 12, and often up to 70 hungry bodies. It is also where regular experiments this year took place on integrating the magical Moringa (grown on site) into nutritional smoothies and flapjacks – new suggested additions to the children's packed lunches. In front of him - adjacent to the netball court and football pitch - goats, pigeons, guinea fowl, turkeys, ducks, rabbits and lots of chickens each have their place and purpose, alongside the masses of sugar cane which protect the avocado, papaya and many other plants growing behind them.

10 years ago, we thought we might help pay the fees of some children, like Eric, who were significantly worse off than ourselves. We thought it might make a small difference to a handful of children. Today it is a project that not only works, but has already substantially changed the lives of many, and the knock-on effects of this are incalculable. It already shows definite signs of long-term sustainability and this year's summer school again showed that it can be as enriching for the volunteers as it clearly is for the children. The project, with the Campus as its hub, works excellently and is ostensibly making a substantial difference to a great many people's lives.

(Today Eric is in university medical school and there are 75 children in the Chifundo Project).

Keen early learners of basic computer skills

Fish

Baked Salmon with Mustard and Honey

Cod with Cherry Tomatoes, Basil and Mozzarella

Cod with Prawns and Vegetable Bake

Lemon Sole with Stilton and Dill

Monkfish, Mushrooms, Chives and Parma Ham

Rasputin Carbonara

Salmon and Leek Tart

Salmon Pasta Bake

Baked Salmon with Mustard and Honey

Serves 4

Ingredients:

sunflower oil
4 x 6oz/175g salmon fillets
2 tblsp grainy mustard
2 tblsp runny honey
½ tblsp chopped dill

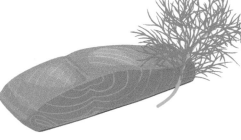

Method:

1. Brush baking sheet with oil and lay salmon fillets skin side down.
2. Mix honey, mustard and dill together. Spoon over the fish.
3. Roast in preheated oven @ 200C for 12 minutes.
4. Serve immediately with baby new potatoes and green vegetable such as broccoli or peas.

*Give a man a fish and you feed him for a day.
Teach a man to fish and you
feed him for a lifetime.*

Early Eastern Sage

Cod with Cherry Tomatoes, Basil and Mozzarella

Serves 2

Ingredients:

2 X 8oz/225g fillets of Cod
olive oil
salt & pepper
8-10 cherry tomatoes
fresh basil
1 ball of buffalo Mozzarella
1 tblsp grated Parmesan cheese

Method:

1. Preheat oven to 220C and place fish on greased roasting tray.
2. Drizzle with olive oil and season well.
3. Place tomatoes, basil and sliced mozzarella on top of fish.
4. Sprinkle with Parmesan and more olive oil and bake till golden for 15-20 minutes.
5. If you can get yellow and red tomatoes they really enhances the look of this dish.

Life can only be understood backwards but it must be lived forwards.

Soren Kierkegaard

Cod with Prawns and Vegetable Bake

Ingredients:

8oz/225g diced carrots

6oz/175g sliced mushrooms

1 red pepper, diced

3 tomatoes, skinned and diced

1oz/25g butter

6oz/175g breadcrumbs

1lb/450g cod or other white fish, skinned and chopped

prawns, use defrosted, cooked prawns (optional)

4oz/150g grated cheddar cheese

1 pint parsley sauce

Method:

1. Melt the butter and slowly cook all the vegetables until soft.
2. Place vegetables in bottom of an ovenproof dish.
3. Mix cod with prawns. Place on top of vegetables.
4. Make up 1 pint parsley sauce (packet or freshly made). Pour sauce over fish.
5. Mix breadcrumbs and cheddar cheese and sprinkle on top.
6. Bake at 155C for 35 minutes or until golden brown on top.

A ship in harbor is safe,
but that is not what ships are built for.

John A. Shedd

Lemon Sole with Stilton & Dill
(2 Servings)

Ingredients:

2 fillets of lemon sole
2-3oz/75g Stilton cheese
fresh or dried dill
seasoning

Method:

1. Pre-heat oven to 200C
2. Halve the fillets of sole lengthwise.
3. Place a knob of Stilton on each piece of fish and roll up.
4. Secure with cocktail stick. Sprinkle generously with chopped dill.
5. Place fish rolls in greased baking dish and cover.
6. Bake for 12 - 15 minutes.
7. Serve with new potatoes and broccoli and carrots.

The best thing about the future is that it comes only one day at a time.

Abraham Lincoln

Monkfish with Mushroom, Chives and Parma Ham

(4 servings)

Ingredients:

1lb/450g monkfish, cut into four pieces
1 tblsp chopped chives
6oz/175g mushrooms finely chopped
8 slices Parma ham
1oz/25g butter
seasoning

Method:

1. Pre-heat oven 200C
2. Cut out four squares of greaseproof paper. Brush with olive oil.
3. Fry mushrooms on high heat in butter till brown.
4. On greaseproof paper place 2 slices of Parma ham. Top with mushrooms and chopped chives and one piece of fish.
5. Roll up each parcel into a roll, then gently remove the paper.
6. Place fish rolls on a greased cooking tray and roast for 15-20 minutes.
7. Fish may be sliced before serving.
8. Serve with mashed potatoes and colourful vegetables.

Life is not a problem to be solved,
but a mystery to be lived.

Richard Rohr

Rasputin Carbonara

Serves 4
Prep 5 minutes - Cook 10 Minutes

Ingredients:

400g spaghetti
2 tsp butter
2 garlic cloves, crushed
10fl.oz/300ml double cream
4 eggs, beaten
3 tblsp freshly grated Parmesan
8oz/240g smoked salmon, shredded
bunch of chives, snipped
salt & pepper

Method:

1. Cut the salmon into small strips.
2. In a small pan, melt the butter and add the garlic and gently sizzle for 1 min. Remove from the heat.
3. In a bowl, lightly beat the cream, eggs, softened garlic and half the Parmesan. Stir in the strips of smoked salmon.
4. Cook the spaghetti and drain well and return the pan to the heat. Add the salmon mixture and the chives, and toss well so the heat from the pasta lightly thickens the sauce. Serve scattered with the remaining Parmesan, season with salt and plenty of black pepper.
5. Serve with Garlic Bread.

Salmon and Leek Tart

Ingredients:
1 sheet ready-made short crust pastry
2oz/50g butter
8 leeks, thinly sliced
1lb/450g salmon, in chunks
Sauce:
2oz/50g butter
2oz/50g flour
1 pint/20fl.oz milk
seasoning

Method:
1. Place the pastry on a greased 11" flan dish and bake blind @ 180C for about 15-20 mins.
2. Heat the butter in a pan, add the leeks and 2 tblsp of water, cover and cook slowly till soft.
3. Melt butter In a pot, add flour and milk to make white sauce.
4. Place salmon chunks in pastry case. Add leeks to sauce mix and season well.
5. Pour sauce over salmon and bake in preheated oven for 25 – 30 minutes until slightly set.
6. Serve at room temperature.

When you feel neglected, think of the female salmon, who lays 3,000,000 eggs but no one remembers her on Mother's Day...

Salmon Pasta Bake

Ingredients:
1 lb/450g penne or fusilli
1 tblsp butter
1 medium onion, sliced
2 garlic cloves, thinly sliced
1 tsp cornflour
14 fl.oz/400 ml milk
4 salmon fillets
2 tblsp chopped chives
2 tsp English mustard
4oz/125g grated Cheddar cheese
salt/ freshly ground pepper

Method:
1. Preheat oven to 200C.
2. Cook pasta according to packet instructions, drain and keep warm.
3. Melt butter in frying pan. Add onion and garlic and cook to soften, and then sprinkle in cornflour. Pour in milk and stir. Bring sauce to boil, stirring continuously for 3 minutes until it thickens.
4. Add the salmon, reduce heat to low and simmer for 5-7minutes. Remove from heat and stir in chives, mustard and half of the cheese.
5. Place fish and sauce into a baking dish with pasta, scatter the remaining cheese on top.
6. Bake in oven for 10 – 15 minutes until cheese is melted and golden. Serve hot.

Pupils at the Summer School with an eye to the future.

Desserts

Almond and Blackberry Tart

Almond and Raspberry Pie

Apple/ Fruits of the Forest or Rhubarb   Crumble

Banoffi Pie

Caramelised Bananas

Chocolate Roulade

Creamy Mango Brulee

Frozen Fruit and White Chocolate Sauce

Ginger Nut Roulade

Instant Strawberry Ice Cream

Lime Flan

Passion Fruit Ice Cream

Pavlova

Pink Lady Strudel

Quick Chocolate Mousse

Simple Lemon Cheesecake

Summer Fruit Brulee

Tiramisu

Almond and Blackberry Tart

Ingredients:

1 packet ready-made shortcrust pastry
4oz/100g caster sugar
4oz/100g soft butter
4oz/100g ground almonds
3 tblsp blackberry or blackcurrant jam
6oz/175g blackberries

Method:

1. Preheat oven to 170C and roll out pastry to fit 23cm. loose bottomed tart tin. Lift pastry into tin trimming off any excess.
2. Prick the base with a fork. Then spoon on and spread the jam over the pastry and refrigerate for about 20 minutes.
3. Blend the eggs, sugar, butter and ground almonds until smooth.
4. Spread the almond mix into the pastry case and place the blackberries on top. Bake for 30-40 minutes until set and golden brown.
5. Serve cold or warm with cream or ice cream.

The Rose is without why
She blooms because she blooms
She does not care for herself
Asks not if she is seen.

Meister Eckharts - The Rose

Almond and Raspberry Pie

(If you have egg yolks over after making a Pavlova
  this is a great way of using them up!)

Ingredients:

4oz/125g butter
4oz/125g sugar
4 medium egg yolks
½ tsp almond essence
4oz/125g ground almonds
1 tblsp plain flour
15-20 raspberries or cherries

Method:

1. Cream the butter and sugar. Beat in the egg yolks
   one at a time, followed by the almond essence.
2. Sift in the flour, fold in almonds until smooth and
   pour into a pie dish approx. 9" x 7"
3. Press raspberries or cherries into the mixture.
4. Cook for approx. 45 minutes or until the pie is risen
   and set.
5. Serve with cream or ice cream.

*Prick an eye and you will draw a tear, prick a
heart and you will bring its feelings to light.*

(Ecc. 22:19)

Apple/Rhubarb
Apple & Fruits of Forest Fruit Crumble

Ingredients:

3/4 stewed apples and frozen Fruits of the Forest
berries or
1 large or 2 small bunches rhubarb, stewed

Crumble:

4ozs/110g brown flour
4oz/110g porridge/oatmeal
5ozs/140g brown sugar
1 tsp baking powder
3ozs/75g butter/marg

Method:

1. Put flour, oatmeal and baking powder in bowl –
   mix with butter till like crumbs or mix in food
   processor. Add sugar and mix well.
2. Put on top of stewed fruit in deep, ovenproof dish
   as during baking fruit will boil up a little.
3. Cook at 180C for 30 – 35 mins. Put cinnamon on
   top if desired.
4. Serve with custard, yogurt or fresh cream.
   Delicious hot or cold.

This crumble mix will freeze well in freezer bags. I make up a large quantity at a time in the food processor. I also stew fruit when I have time to spare and keep in freezer. Then you only have to defrost both and sprinkle the crumble on top of fruit and cook while having your main course.

Thousands of candles can be lighted
from a single candle
And the life of the candle will not be shortened.
Happiness never decreases by being shared.

Buddha

Banoffi Pie

serves 8

Ingredients:

8oz/200g digestive biscuits
4oz/100g butter
4 bananas
1 tin of Carnation caramel
½ pint/275 ml whipped cream
grated chocolate

Method:

1. Crush biscuits and mix with melted butter. Press into base and up sides of 23cm spring form tin. Chill for 15 minutes.
2. Spread the caramel over the base gently with a spoon. Arrange the banana slices on top.
3. Spoon the cream over the bananas and finish with grated chocolate.

Wisdom begins with wonder.

Socrates

Caramelised Bananas

Ingredients:

2oz/50g butter
2oz/50g brown sugar
8floz/250ml pineapple/apple juice
2 tblsp lime juice
6-8 small bananas or 4 regular bananas
(peeled and cut in half lengthwise)

Method:

1. Melt the butter till it bubbles. Add sugar, apple juice and lime juice. Cook over high heat till syrupy, 8 – 10 minutes.
2. Reduce heat to medium, add bananas for 3-4 minutes until slightly softened, turning gently with tongs to cook both sides.
3. Serve bananas with sauce, and frozen yogurt/ice cream/cream.

*Life does not change by chance,
it gets better by change.*

Richard Rohr

Chocolate Roulade

Ingredients:

6 eggs
8oz/225g caster sugar
½ tsp vanilla essence
2oz/50 g cocoa, sifted twice
1oz/25g finely grated chocolate
sifted icing sugar
8floz/300 ml cream

Method:

1. Heat oven to 140C and line a Swiss roll tin (33x21 cm/12"x 9") with parchment paper.
2. Whisk egg yolks, vanilla and sugar till pale and fluffy. Fold in cocoa with metal spoon.
3. With a clean whisk, beat egg whites till stiff. Fold one spoonful into cocoa mixture to loosen, then fold in the rest with firm and fast strokes.
4. Pour into tin and bake for 20 mins, till springy. Turn out onto parchment paper sprinkled with icing sugar and leave to cool for a while. Before fully cold, roll up with paper.
5. When cold, fill with whipped sweetened cream and raspberries (optional) and roll gently. Cracking may occur but adds to the homemade look.

The key to everything is patience You get the chicken by hatching the egg, not smashing it.

Andrew H Glasgow

Creamy Mango Brulee

Ingredients:

2 mangoes
9oz/250g Mascarpone cheese
7floz/200 ml/ Greek-style yogurt
1 tsp ground ginger
zest & juice of 1 lime
2 tblsp soft, light brown sugar
4 tblsp demerara sugar or enough to cover the top of each ramekin

Method:

1. Peel, slice and chop the mangoes and divide between 4 ramekins.
2. Beat the mascarpone cheese with the yogurt, fold in ginger, lime zest and juice and soft brown sugar.
3. Divide this mixture into the ramekins. Chill for two hours.
4. Sprinkle 2 tblsp of demerara sugar over each ramekin and allow to caramelise under hot grill for 2/3 minutes. Cool and chill till required. Eat on same day.

*Let kindliness and loyalty never leave you:
tie them round your neck.*

Book of Proverbs

Frozen Fruit with White Chocolate Sauce

Serves 6

Ingredients:

1 packet of frozen Fruits of the Forest
½ pint cream
1 large bar white chocolate

Method:

1. Early in the day bring fruits to the boil and allow cool.
2. Near serving time warm fruit to tepid.
3. Over a pot of boiling water melt the chocolate and stir in the cream.
4. Divide the fruits into pretty glasses and cover with the melted chocolate and cream.
5. Serve immediately.

There is more to life than simply increasing its speed.

Mahatma Gandhi

Ginger Nut Roulade

Ingredients:

1 packet ginger nut biscuits
1 mug strong coffee
½ pint whipped cream
chocolate flake or grated chocolate

Method:

1. Pour cooled coffee into a bowl.
2. Take biscuits one at a time and dip into the coffee. Put spoon of whipped cream on biscuit and sandwich moist biscuits together with cream to form a log.
3. Stand upright on a plate as you go. Continue until all biscuits are lined up on the plate.
4. Cover the log with remaining cream. Sprinkle with grated chocolate or chocolate flake.
5. Refrigerate till ready to serve – best eaten 24 hours after making to allow biscuits to soften.

*A man is but the product of his thoughts,
what he thinks he becomes.*

Mahatma Gandhi

Instant Strawberry Ice Cream

Ingredients:

12 – 14 frozen strawberries
1 ramekin of sugar
1 cup buttermilk
2 tsp vanilla essence

Method:

Need food processor with steel bowl or ice crusher as
frozen strawberries may crack plastic bowl!

1. Put everything together into food processor and
   pulse for approx. 2 minutes.
2. Can be served immediately but if not using
   immediately put into freezer in container.
3. Quantities can be doubled or trebled for a summer
   BBQ dessert.

Earth's crammed with heaven,
and every common bush afire with God:
But only he who sees, takes off his shoes,
the rest of us just sit around and
pluck blackberries...

Elizabeth Barrett Browning (1806-1861)

Lime Flan

Ingredients:

For the base:
15 Digestive biscuits
3oz/70g butter
1oz/25g brown sugar

Topping:
zest and juice of 3-4 limes
1 can full-fat condensed milk
15floz/450ml double cream

Method:

1. Crush the biscuits finely, add sugar and melted butter and press into the base of 23cm loose bottomed tin.
2. Combine lime juice, condensed milk and cream and beat till well mixed.
3. Fold in ¾ of the lime zest with a spoon.
4. Pour the filling over the biscuit base and smooth the top.
5. Refrigerate till ready to serve and sprinkle with remaining zest.
6. This is best eaten on the day it is made as biscuit may soften if left too long.

If we move even the smallest step out of our limitations, life comes to embrace us and lead us into the pastures of possibility.

John O'Donohue – Eternal Echoes

Passion Fruit Ice Cream

Ingredients:

4 crushed meringues
½ pint/10floz cream
10oz/300g jar lemon curd
4 passion fruits

Method:

1. Whip the cream to soft peaks.
2. Fold in the Lemon Curd, add in the meringues and pulp of passion fruits.
3. Spoon into a 1lb loaf tin lined with 2 layers of cling film. Freeze overnight.
4. Turn out and slice. Serve with extra passion fruit if liked.
5. So handy to have in the freezer for unexpected guests.

Love is a fruit in season at all times,
and within the reach of every hand.

Saint Teresa of Calcutta

Pavlova

Ingredients:
4 eggs
8oz/225g caster sugar
1 level tsp cornflour
1 level tsp white wine vinegar

Method:
1. Preheat fan oven to 130C and line a baking tray with baking parchment.
2. Whisk egg whites in grease free bowl till stiff and peaking.
3. While still beating, add caster sugar, 1 teaspoonful at a time.
4. Mix together cornflour and vinegar and dribble into mix while beating.
5. Spread the meringue into a circle on the tray, leaving sides a little higher.
6. Bake for about 1 hour and allow cool in the oven.
7. When cool fill with ½ pint whipped cream and fruit of your choice.

People travel to wonder at the height of the mountains, at the huge waves of the seas, at the long course of the rivers, at the vast compass of the earth, at the circular motion of the stars, and yet they pass by themselves without wondering.

Saint Augustine

Pink Lady Strudel

Ingredients:
1 pkt. frozen puff pastry
3 Pink Lady apples
2 tblsp brown sugar
a little butter
1 egg, beaten with a splash of whole milk
icing sugar to dust (optional)

Method:
1. Preheat oven to 200C.
2. Peel, quarter, core and thinly slice the apples and mix in a bowl with 1 tblsp of sugar.
3. Grease an oblong baking tray with butter.
4. Lay pastry on surface with wider side facing you.
5. Brush the pastry with egg wash, scatter apples evenly over it, leaving a little room around the edge.
6. Tightly roll the pastry away from you.
7. Pinch edges together and brush with egg wash, sprinkle with sugar.
8. Bake for about 20 minutes, dust with icing sugar and serve with cream.

This is in fact much easier to make than an Apple Tart and ever so tasty!

*Millions saw the apple fall,
but Newton was the only one who asked why.*

Bernard Baruch

Quick Chocolate Mousse

Ingredients:

8oz/225g plain chocolate, broken in pieces
4 eggs, separated
1 tblsp rum
1 knob butter
¼ pint double cream, lightly whipped
To finish: whipped cream and grated chocolate

Method:

1. Place chocolate in bowl over gently simmering water to melt.
2. Remove from heat and stir in egg yolks one at a time.
3. Add rum and butter. Fold in cream until evenly blended.
4. Beat egg whites until stiff, and fold into chocolate mixture.
5. Pour into dish or individual dishes and chill until set.
6. Decorate with whipped cream and chocolate curls.

This mousse freezes well and needs 4 hours to thaw. Decorate after defrosting.

*If you judge people,
you have no time to love them.*

Saint Mother Teresa

Simple Lemon Cheesecake

Ingredients:

6oz/175g digestive biscuits, crushed
3oz/75g butter, melted
1 tin Carnation Light Condensed Milk
10oz/300g tub light cream cheese
zest and juice of 2 lemons

You will also need...
20cm (8 inch) loose-bottomed cake tin

Method:

1. Tip the biscuit crumbs into a bowl, add melted butter and mix in. Spoon into the tin and press down to level. Chill for 10 minutes.
2. Pour the condensed milk into a large bowl. Add the light cheese and whisk together. Mix in the lemon juice and zest (watch it thicken!). Pour into the tin. Chill for 2-4 hours or until set.
3. To serve, remove the cheesecake from the tin and decorate with berries or 2tblsp lemon curd warmed with a little water and drizzled on top.

Live simply, so that others can simply live.

Mahatma Gandhi

Summer Fruit Brulee

Ingredients:

8oz/200g strawberries and 4oz/100g raspberries
12oz/350g fromage frais
2oz/50g brown sugar
2 dsp caster sugar

Method:

1. Chop strawberries and sprinkle caster sugar on top.
2. Divide strawberries and raspberries between four ramekins.
3. Spoon fromage frais over the fruit.
4. Sprinkle brown sugar on top and caramelise with blow torch or under hot grill.

Strive not to be a success, but to be of value.

Albert Einstein

Tiramisu with Baileys and Coffee

Serves 6 – 8 and best made the day before

Ingredients:

7oz/200g Lady Fingers (Boudoir biscuits)
jug of strong lukewarm coffee (de-caff. if you wish)
7fl.oz/250ml whipped cream
9oz/250g Mascarpone cheese (1tub)
4floz/100ml Baileys Irish Cream Liqueur
2oz/50g caster sugar
Garnish – whipped cream and cocoa

Method:

1. Mix together Baileys, sugar and cheese till well blended and then fold in about two thirds of the whipped cream. Set aside.
2. Lay a layer of biscuits on bottom of dish or individual glasses.
    Drizzle with coffee till biscuits are moist.
3. Spread half of the Baileys mixture on top of biscuits and sprinkle with sieved cocoa.
4. Add another layer of biscuits and drizzle with coffee. Again cover with balance of Baileys mixture and sprinkle with sieved cocoa.
5. Top with remaining whipped cream and sprinkle with grated chocolate. Allow 24 hours before serving for allow biscuits to absorb flavours.

Lovely made in Martini glasses or other glass dishes for individual helpings.

Quite a heavy dessert so a small helping is plenty! A great dessert with no cooking involved!

The unexamined life is not worth living.
Socrates

High kicks near the Chicken House

Baking

Almond Slices

Basic Biscuit Recipe

Boiled Fruit Cake

Brown Bread

Chocolate Cake/ Muffins

Chocolate Chip Cookies

Claire's Coffee Cake

Coconut Macaroons

Coffee Shop Scones

Fruit Brack

Fruity Chocolate Biscuits

Lemon Drizzle Tray Bake

Lemon Shortbread Biscuits

Meringues

Muffins

Orange and Lemon Tasty Bites

Pear and Almond Sponge

White Chocolate & Raspberry Tray Bake

Almond Slices

Ingredients:

1 sheet of readymade shortcrust pastry
2 tblsp raspberry jam
4oz/100g butter
4oz/100g caster sugar
2 eggs
few drops almond essence
3oz/75g ground almonds
1oz/25g plain flour
2oz/50g flaked almonds

Method:

1. Heat oven to 180C and line a greased Swiss roll tin with pastry, spread with jam.
2. Cream butter and sugar, beat in eggs, add almond essence, and fold in ground almonds and flour. Mix well.
3. Spread the mixture evenly over the tin and sprinkle with flaked almonds.
4. Bake for 30 – 35 minutes.
5. Cut into finger size slices to serve.

The purpose of our lives is to be happy.
Dalai Lama

Basic Biscuit Recipe

Ingredients:

6oz/175g flour
4oz/110g soft butter
2oz/50g caster sugar
flavouring.
Heat oven to 180C

Method:

1. Put flour in a bowl and rub in soft butter till well mixed.
2. Add sugar and bring to stiff dough. Add flavouring.
3. Roll out to ¼" thickness and cut into shapes as required.
4. Place on cooking tray and cook 7 – 10 mins.
5. You may flavour the basic biscuits with cinnamon, ginger, lemon zest etc.

Whoever is happy will make others happy too.

Anne Frank

Boiled Fruit Cake

Ingredients:
5oz/140g butter, cubed
6oz/175g light muscovado sugar
10.5oz/300g plain flour
2 tsp baking powder
2 tsp mixed spice
2 eggs, lightly beaten
8.5 fl.oz/250 ml orange juice
1 pkt. of luxury fruit mix

Method:
1. Preheat oven to 160C and line a 20cm cake tin with baking paper.
2. Put butter, sugar, orange juice and dried fruits into large saucepan and bring slowly to the boil, stirring to melt the butter, reduce the heat and simmer for 10 mins.
3. Leave until almost cold then sift the flour, baking powder and spices into the saucepan and add the eggs and stir all the ingredients together.
4. Spoon the mixture into the tin and bake in oven for 1¼ -1½ hours until cooked. Leave to cool in tin for 15 mins and then turn out onto a wire rack and cool completely.

*Education is not the filling of a pail,
but the lighting of a fire.*

William Butler Yeats

Brown Bread Recipe

4 loaves (just the easiest brown bread to make)

Ingredients:

1½lbs/675g coarse wholemeal flour
1 pint buttermilk
½ lb/225g plain flour
1 pint water
3 tsp salt and sugar
6ozs/175g porridge oats
4 tsp bread soda
Any other seeds you wish or pinhead oatmeal, wheat
    germ etc. may be added.

Method:

1. Heat oven to 210C.
2. Sieve together plain flour with bread soda.
3. Add all other dry ingredients – mix well.
4. Pour over milk and water. Stir well to moisten all
   dry ingredients.
5. Divide mixture between 4 greased 1 lb. loaf tins.
6. Put knife mark down centre of loaves and bake for
   40-45 minutes.

There are some people in the world so hungry,
that God cannot appear to them except in the
form of bread.

Gandhi

Chocolate Cake
Makes 1 (or 15 Muffins)

Ingredients:

6oz/175g plain flour
6oz/175g dark brown sugar
6oz/175g soft margarine
2 level tsp baking powder
1½ heaped tblsp cocoa (blended in hot water, to
    dropping consistency, then cooled).
3 eggs
2 x 8" tins well-greased. Heat oven 200C.

Method:

1. Put all ingredients in bowl and blend together with
   minimum of beating.
2. If any cocoa is left in bowl, rinse with 1 tsp of water and add to mixture.
3. Divide mixture into 2 tins and cook in preheated
   oven 25 minutes.

Filling/icing:

3 tblsp milk
2oz/50g hard margarine/butter
1 heaped tblsp cocoa
5oz/150g icing sugar

1. Dissolve all ingredients together. Beat in icing sugar until consistency is such it won't flow off cake. This will take minimum of 5-6oz icing sugar.
2. This can be used to ice the muffins or to fill and ice the two cakes.

Nature is pleased with simplicity.
And nature is no dummy.

Isaac Newton

Chocolate Chip Cookies

35 cookies approx

Ingredients:

2oz/50g margarine
2oz/50g castor Sugar
2oz/50g brown sugar
1 egg
½ tsp vanilla essence
4oz/100g self-raising flour
6oz/150g chocolate chips or plain chocolate

Method:

1. Preheat oven to 190C.
2. In a large mixing bowl, cream the margarine with castor sugar and brown sugar until fluffy.
3. Add the egg and a little bit of flour and then stir in the vanilla essence.
4. Sieve in the flour and stir in the chocolate chips.
5. Drop rounded teaspoonfuls onto a greased tray. Leave plenty of room between them as they will spread.
6. Bake for 8-10 minutes. Cool on a rack. Keep in a tin for freshness.

Our greatest glory is not in never falling, but in rising every time we fall.

Confucius

Claire's Coffee Cake

Ingredients:
8oz/225g soft margarine
8oz/225g self-raising flour
8oz/225g caster sugar
4 eggs
4 tblsp Camp coffee essence
2oz/50g chopped walnuts (optional)
1 tsp baking powder

Method:
1. Grease 2 x 8" round cake tins
2. Preheat oven to175C.
3. Put all ingredients in a bowl and beat well.
4. Divide between 2 greased tins.
5. Bake for 20-25 minutes @ 175C.

Filling: 3oz/75g butter, 6oz/175g icing sugar, 3 tsp Camp coffee essence.
Beat together and sandwich between two cakes.

For smaller cake in 7" tins:
1. Use 6oz of all ingredients instead of 8oz and 3 tblsp of Coffee Essence and 3 eggs.
2. Also works well as tray bake with filling on top as icing.

Either you run the day or the day runs you.

Jim Rohn

Coconut Macaroons

Approx. 40

Ingredients:

1 tin Carnation Condensed Milk
14oz/400g desiccated coconut
1 tsp vanilla or almond extract
4oz/115g dark chocolate (optional)
You will also need:
2 large greased and parchment-lined baking sheets

Method:

1. Preheat the oven to 140C.
2. Mix together the condensed milk, coconut and vanilla extract in a large bowl.
3. Drop rounded teaspoonfuls onto the prepared baking sheets.
4. Bake for 15-20 minutes or until turning brown at the edges. Allow to cool for 5 minutes before transferring to a wire rack to cool completely.

Optional Chocolate Drizzle: Melt the dark chocolate in the microwave and place half in a small bowl. Dip the base of each biscuit into the chocolate, then place back onto the tray to set. Use the remaining melted chocolate to drizzle over the macaroons.

*What we become
depends on the choices we make.*

Jean Shinoda Bolen

Coffee Shop Scones

Ingredients:
1lb/450g self-raising flour
1 tsp baking powder
pinch of salt
4oz/110g margarine
3-4oz/100g caster sugar
1 egg
3-4 tblsp cream (optional)
7-8 floz/275ml milk

Method:
1. Pre-heat oven to 200C. Sieve together flour, baking powder and salt. Chop margarine into chunks and add.
2. Either put the mix into food processor and mix till like fine breadcrumbs or mix with pastry blender.
3. Beat egg and milk together and stir into dry mix.
4. Toss dough on lightly floured board and gently form into a ball
5. Roll into circle about 1" high and cut into shapes with knife or scone cutter.
6. Meanwhile heat lightly floured baking tray in oven.
7. Remove tray and place scones on heated tray and bake 14-18 minutes depending on size of scones.
8. Cool on a wired rack.

*We cannot all do great things,
but we can do small things with great love.*

Saint Mother Teresa of Calcutta.

Fruity Chocolate Biscuits

(Approx.24)

Ingredients:

250g/8oz butter
150g/5oz sugar
150g/5oz self-raising flour
225g/7oz porridge oats
200g/7oz glacé cherries/dried cranberries
50g/2oz white chocolate buttons, chopped
Preheat oven to 180°C/Gas mark 4

Method:

1. Line 2 or 3 baking sheets with baking parchment.
2. Beat the butter and sugar until light and fluffy. Stir in the flour and oats, mix well. Chop the cherries/cranberries roughly and stir these and the white chocolate buttons into the mixture.
3. Divide the mixture into 24 equal pieces. Roll each piece into a small ball. Put on the lined baking sheet and press down. Allow plenty of space between each cookie to allow them spread.
4. Bake in the pre heated oven for 15 -17 minutes or until cookies are pale gold around the edge but still soft in the middle. Allow to cool on the baking sheet for 5 minutes and then transfer to a wire rack.

Note:

If storing uncooked mixture in the fridge, roll into a log and wrap in baking parchment and cling film. One of the things that make these cookies extra special is that the mixture keeps uncooked in the fridge for a week so you can bake a few fresh, warm cookies at a time. It also freezes uncooked for 6 months.

To be able to look back on one's life in satisfaction, is to live twice.

Kahlil Gibran

Fruit Brack

Ingredients:
8oz/225g dried fruit
1 large cup boiling water
8oz/225g plain flour
1 tsp bread soda
I egg
4oz/110g brown sugar

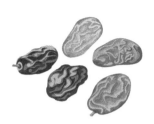

Method:
1. Soak the fruit in the boiling water till cool.
2. Add 1 tsp bread soda and stir.
3. Add beaten egg to this mixture and mix well.
4. Stir in the sugar followed by the flour. Mix well.
5. Put into greased 1 lb. loaf tin and bake at 180C for about 1 hour.

Tip: I usually make two at a time in different bowls. Delicious sliced with butter and lovely toasted after a few days.

Well, I must endure the presence of a few caterpillars if I wish to become acquainted with the butterflies.

Antoine de Saint-Exupéry, The Little Prince

Lemon Drizzle Traybake

Ingredients:
8oz/225g margarine
8oz/225g caster sugar
10oz/275g self-raising flour
2 tsp baking powder
4 large eggs
4 tblsp milk
zest of 2 lemons

Drizzle ingredients: juice 2 lemons
6oz/175g sugar

Method:
1. Grease and line base and sides of baking tin (21cm X 30cm) with parchment.
2. Beat all ingredients, other than lemon juice, together till smooth.
3. Pour into the prepared tin, levelling the top.
4. Bake in oven for 35 – 40 minutes at 140C.
5. Allow cake to cool in tin for about 10 minutes. Turn out carefully onto wire rack.
6. Mix together juice of 2 lemons with 6oz/175g of sugar and drizzle on top of cake.
7. When cool cut into squares.

How wonderful it is that nobody need wait a single moment before starting to improve the world.

Anne Frank

Lemon Shortbread Biscuits

Ingredients:

6oz/170g flour
2oz/50g caster sugar
finely grated zest of 1 lemon
4oz/110g butter in small cubes
icing sugar to serve

Method:

1. Preheat oven to 180C.
2. Put flour, caster sugar, lemon zest and butter cubes in food processor.
3. Whizz until combined.
4. Roll out dough to about 1cm/1/2" thick and cut into shapes.
5. Bake on a tray for 6 -8 minutes.
6. Leave to cool slightly on the tray, then remove to wire rack.

*It is not how much we have,
but how much we enjoy that makes happiness.*

Gandhi

Meringues

Ingredients:
4 egg whites
8oz/225g caster sugar

Method:
1. Line large tray with parchment paper and preheat oven to 150C.
2. Whisk egg whites till really stiff in a clean dry bowl.
3. Keep beating egg whites while adding the sugar.
4. Fold in the last ounce of caster sugar with a metal spoon.
5. Put spoonfuls onto tray and bake for approx.1 hour. Meringues will keep in a tin for couple of weeks.

You can never cross the ocean until you have the courage to lose sight of the shore.

Christopher Columbus

Muffins

Ingredients:
Ilb/450g self-raising flour
8oz/225g caster sugar
8oz/225g margarine
2 eggs, beaten
1 tsp baking powder
7floz/225ml milk

Method:
1. Preheat oven to 180C. Lay 20-24 cases in muffin tins.
2. Heat milk and margarine over a pot of water till melted, set aside to cool.
3. Mix flour, caster sugar and baking powder together in a large bowl.
4. Make a well in flour mixture, then add the beaten eggs and milk/marg. mixture and beat well.
5. Add your own chosen additions: 6oz/175g chocolate chips or 7oz/200g raspberries halved or blueberries, finely chopped apple with cinnamon or 1 pear, peeled and finely chopped.
6. With two dessert spoons fill the muffin cases and bake for 20-25 minutes.

Tip: Raspberry or chocolate are generally the favourites. It's easy to divide the finished mixture and make both varieties!

It is never too late to become what you might have been.

George Eliot

Orange and Lemon Tasty Bites

Ingredients:

2oz/50g breadcrumbs

8oz/200g caster sugar

4oz/100g ground almonds

1½ tsp baking powder

7floz/200ml sunflower oil

4 eggs

zest of 1 orange and 1 lemon

Drizzle:

juice of 1 lemon and 1orange

3oz/75g caster sugar

Method:

1. Mix all above ingredients and pour into a greased Swiss roll tin.
2. Place in a cold oven and then turn heat to 180C. Cook 45 – 60 minutes.
3. When cool, heat orange and lemon juice with caster sugar and bring to boil.
4. Drizzle evenly over the cake.
5. Cut into 12 portions or 60 cubes.
6. These will not rise but remain moist and very tasty.

A divided orange tastes just as good.

Book of Proverbs

Pear and Almond Sponge

Ingredients:

6oz/150g soft margarine
6oz/150g caster sugar
1 tsp almond essence
3 eggs
2oz/50g ground almonds
8oz/225g self-raising flour
1 tin pear halves

Method:

1. Butter an ovenproof dish or spring form tin.
2. Drain the pears and allow to dry on kitchen paper.
3. Cream margarine, sugar and almond essence.
4. Beat in eggs and fold in flour, ground almonds and 1 or 2 of the pear halves, finely chopped.
5. Put mix into tin and gently place finely sliced remaining pears on top.
6. Bake at 180C for 35 - 40 minutes till well risen. Serve with whipped cream.

Use what talents you possess: The woods would be very silent if no birds sang there except those who sang best.

Henry Van Dyke

White Chocolate & Raspberry Tray Bake

12-18 pieces

Ingredients:
7oz/200g soft margarine
pinch of salt
7oz/200g caster sugar
2oz/50g ground almonds
4 medium eggs
4oz/125g raspberries
1 tsp vanilla extract
4oz/100g white chocolate, chopped
7oz/200g self-raising flour
icing sugar to dust

Method:
1. Preheat oven to 180C and grease a 12"x6" tray with butter and baking paper.
2. Cream the margarine and sugar well and add the eggs, one by one, and vanilla and beat well.
3. Sift the flour and salt and beat into mixture. Fold in the ground almonds and raspberries and chocolate.
4. Pour into prepared tin and bake 45 minutes until skewer comes out clean.
5. Cool in tin, cut into small squares and sprinkle with icing sugar.

We can believe what we choose. We are answerable for what we choose to believe.

St. John Henry Newman

Reflection from a First Time Volunteer

"Why are you doing it?" He asked.
Because I want to! My friend's question is valid... and has stayed with me for 6 weeks since he pricked my conscience. Now with less than a week to go, I wonder. "Why am I heading off to teach the children in Malawi in July?"

These children are poor, but then what does poor mean? They live in houses with a mud floor, most cannot read or write. Their families may earn as little as fifty euros a month, yet petrol costs the same is it does here.

I don't have much but I have more than I need. These children don't have anything and need more than that. I'm no mathematician but it would appear that I have something to give. If I was in need would these children come to my aid? They don't know that I exist and do not have the means. I know they exist and I have the means!

Why am I doing it? Because I can help do something that might make a difference and most of all, because these children want someone who wants to make a difference. Or so I have been told....

I want to go so I can spend time with my friend. He's a teacher in a foreign land. I want to hear his stories from that land as he teaches the children of Chifundo. A week of memories to last us past the next wedding or stag is what I want.

"How much money do you give to charity each year"? my friend asked his parents. They totted it up and realized if they pooled their resources they could do something together. They asked a friend in Malawi what they could do with this money and the response was simple....education. The Chifundo Foundation started by sponsoring 5 children through primary school in 2007. Today they have 75 children some in university, secondary and primary and much more...

How you can help?

You can send a donation now to:

Chifundo Bank Account:
Bank of Ireland, Deansgrange, Co. Dublin
Beneficiary Name: **Chifundo Foundation CLG**
Account Number: **90479114**
Sort Code: **90 11 83**
Swift address: **BOFIIE2D**
IBAN: **IE43 BOFI 9011 8390 4791 14**

or

Donate directly on our website:
www.chifundo.org/donate

or

simply click the PayPal button

or

By cheque to:
Chifundo Foundation CLG,
66 Mount Albany,
Blackrock, Co. Dublin

CPSIA information can be obtained
at www.ICGtesting.com
Printed in the USA
BVHW021412070921
616214BV00016B/795

9 781838 156626